Some Babies Grow Up To Be
COWBOYS

D1603575

Other books in the Western Life Series:

Number One: *Catch Rope—The Long Arm of the Cowboy*
by John Erickson

Number Two: *Through Time and the Valley*
by John Erickson

Number Three: *LZ Cowboy: A Cowboy's Journal 1979–1981*
by John Erickson

Number Four: *Panhandle Cowboy*
by John Erickson

Some Babies Grow Up To Be COWBOYS

A COLLECTION OF ARTICLES AND ESSAYS

By
JOHN R. ERICKSON

Volume 5
Western Life Series

University of North Texas Press
Denton, Texas

The paper in this book meets the minimum requirements of the
American National Standard for Permanence of Paper for Printed
Library Materials, Z39.48.1984.

Permissions
University of North Texas Press
P. O. Box 311336
Denton TX 76203-1336
940-565-2142

Number Five: Western Life Series

Library of Congress Cataloging-in-Publication Data

Erickson, John R. 1943–
Some babies grow up to be cowboys : a collection of articles and essays /
by John R. Erickson.—1st ed.
p.   cm. — (Western life series ; 5)
Includes index.
ISBN 1-57441-120-9
1. Cowboys—Texas—Texas Panhandle—Social life and customs. 2. Ranch life—
Texas—Texas Panhandle. 3. Texas Panhandle (Tex.)—Social life and customs.
4. Ranching—Texas—Texas Panhandle—History. I. Title. II. Series.
F392.P168 E77   1999
976.4'063'088636—dc21
00-008287

Design by Angela Schmitt
Front cover photograph by Kris Erickson

To Frances B. Vick,
Director of the University of North Texas Press
Much deserved

Contents

Part VII: This and That

Preface

MY INTEREST IN RANCH life is probably genetic. My mother's people were Texas frontiersmen, ranchers, and cowboys back to 1858. I had a great-great grandmother who was killed by Comanche Indians in 1860, and is now resting in Willow Springs Cemetery near Weatherford. My great-grandfather, a rancher in Gaines County, was shot and killed by his neighbor in 1917, in a dispute over a waterhole. One of his sons, Uncle Bert Sherman, stayed a bachelor and spent his life working as a cowboy on ranches near Lubbock, while another son, Uncle Roy, lived out his days raising cattle on the Sherman ranch in Gaines County.

My mother's father, Buck Curry, managed a 64,000 acre ranch for many years, and eventually put together an 8,500 acre ranch of his own in Gaines County. He died when I was very young and I have only a few memories of him. I wish I had known him better, for there have been times when I've felt a great kinship with him. He loved guns, spurs, horses, and ranching, and also assembled a huge library on a wide range of subjects. During the 1920s, when cattle rustlers were a scourge to ranchers, he slept with a .41 Colt pistol under his pillow. He was once bitten by a horse suspected of having rabies, and had to endure the treatment of the time—a series of twenty painful injections in the belly, said to be only slightly better than the disease.

He was respected in his community, yet he seemed to revel in being unconventional. He kept a stuffed rattlesnake in his office, and went out in public wearing a coyote-skin coat, probably made of skins he had tanned himself. He had friends among the local ranching aristocracy, but according to my mother, his best friend was a disreputable old scarecrow who trapped skunks for a living—a man my grandmother wouldn't allow in her house because of his smell.

My mother, Anna Beth Curry Erickson, was a wonderful storyteller, and I was raised on her tales of Grampy Buck, Joe Sherman, and Uncles Roy and Bert. At a young age I wanted to be a rancher and a cowboy, and that proved to be such a powerful fantasy that even six years of university education didn't erase it. Between 1974 and 1981 I made my living as a cowboy on ranches in the Texas and Oklahoma Panhandles, and in 1990 Kris and I began putting together our own M-Cross Ranch, named after the brand Great-grandfather Sherman used on his ranches on the South Plains. It is a commercial cow-calf operation in Roberts and Ochiltree Counties, and has grown to 8,500 acres—oddly, the same size as Buck Curry's outfit. I operate it myself, with help from family, neighbors, and part-time cowboy labor.

So, yes, this passion I have for ranch life and cowboying is probably genetic. It is a subject I care deeply about, the lens through which I view the universe and the modern world. And it is, to one degree or another, the subject of all the articles in this collection, which made their first appearances in *Texas Highways, Oklahoma Today, Livestock Weekly, The Dallas Morning News, The Dallas Times-Herald,* and *American Cowboy.* Many of these pieces are anecdotal, based on my experiences and observations on ranches. Others required a fair amount of research and would have to be described as historical. And others fall into the category of "thought pieces," or essays, in which I view contemporary life through the lens of cowboying.

A glance at the table of contents will reveal that I have tried to arrange the articles in a kind of order, starting with several pieces about my place in this world—the Texas Panhandle—and moving into a historical view of the ranching business. This is followed by a section on the cowboy, four articles which probe the same topic from slightly different perspectives. Next we have Cowboy Tools, Ranch and Rodeo, and a section on animals. Several pieces didn't fit any of these categories, so I placed them in the final section, a catch-all grouping called This and That.

After Kris and I were married in 1967, we loaded our belongings into a Volkswagen and drove from Dallas to Boston, where I was a second-year student at Harvard Divinity School. Neither of us could have predicted the twists and turns our trail would follow in years to come, or that it would lead us back to Texas and to the log house we now occupy in Picket Canyon. It has been a wonderful adventure and a partnership every step of the way. In the following pages, Kris isn't often mentioned, but neither do I dwell on the importance of oxygen in my life. Let it be noted that without Kris, none of this would have been worth doing or writing about.

Part I

A Place

The Quakers of Estacado and Their Precious Books

1994

MY COUSINS AND I used to joke that when our grandmother, Mabel Curry, went to heaven, God would call her "Mrs. Curry," and she would address him as "Young Man."

She lived in a gleaming white clapboard house in Seminole, Texas, shaded on all sides by huge elms and pines she had nursed through droughts and dirtstorms. Beyond her white cinder block fence, one saw red sandy soil and wilting mesquites and the vast sweep of the Llano Estacado.

Inside the fence, she imposed her will upon the land and made it green. She and the elements of West Texas slugged it out for eighty-four years, and West Texas certainly met its match in Mrs. B. B. Curry, my mother's mother.

She was every inch a proper lady, but beneath the lace and muslin she was made of steel. Those were the traits of her Quaker forebears, the Underhills from Huron County, Ohio. In 1880 they left green and fertile lands in Ohio and followed Reverend Paris Cox to Crosby County, Texas.

Until they came and established the town of Estacado, no one had ever tried to build a permanent settlement on the Staked Plains above the caprock. The Comanches had learned to survive on the Llano, with its harsh climate and forbidding emptiness, but not even they had tried to make a home of it.

But that's what the Quakers set out to do. They came with plows and seeds and their precious books. Before the modern cities of Lubbock, Plainview, Snyder, and Amarillo had even been thought of, Estacado had a church, a court house, a library society, and was the seat of government for a six-county area of West Texas.

Whatever possessed these quiet, studious people to settle in such an unlikely place? Perhaps they had suffered persecution for their pacifist views during the Civil War. Perhaps they just wanted to be alone, apart from the world, free to pursue their vision of correct living and raise their children in a place that was beyond the corrupting influence of "The Gentiles," as they called those who were not of their faith.

Grandmother Curry's mother, Perlina Underhill, grew to womanhood in Estacado and attended the Quaker school. In *A History of Crosby County, Texas*, "Memories of Estacado," she is quoted as saying: "This school was called an academy and pupils were prepared for college work. French, Latin and German were taught, as I recall."

The Quakers may have prepared their children for college, but there was not a college, or much of anything else, within three hundred miles of Estacado.

In 1887 Perlina met a young cowboy named Joe Sherman who had drifted west from Palo Pinto County. They were married that same year in Estacado, in a Quaker service performed by Reverend Anson Cox.

Lina could hardly have picked a man more Texan and less Quaker than Joe Sherman. Orphaned on the Texas frontier, raised by cowboys on the Loving ranch in Jack County, educated on trail drives to Kansas and Nebraska, he was a man of action and few words.

Grandmother Curry often said, "If Father hadn't been exposed to the good influences of a strong Quaker woman, he probably would have been an outlaw." Perhaps it was Lina who encouraged him to read. Until he died in 1917, he subscribed to the St. Louis Post-Dispatch and kept a book of Shakespeare's plays beside his bed.

When Grandmother Curry was born in Estacado in 1888, her father was employed as a deputy sheriff in a huge jurisdiction that included Crosby, Lubbock, Dickens, and Floyd Counties. But he had come West for land, and in 1890 he moved his young family to a ranch near what is now the town of Shallowater, just north of present day Lubbock.

A year later, in February of 1891, Joe Sherman was one of a handful of men present when Lubbock County was officially organized. I'm sure that none of them ever dreamed that a hundred years later, Lubbock would be the "Hub City of the South Plains," with a population of 180,000.

The Shermans ranched in Lubbock County for fifteen years, and during that time their family grew to seven children, Mabel being the oldest. But by 1905 Joe Sherman had begun losing cattle to rustlers who were changing his M Cross brand into an MB, and he decided to move his operations to a ranch in Gaines County.

I remember Grandmother Curry talking about that cattle drive. It was the kind of adventure a child would never forget. Joe Sherman mounted six of his seven children on horses, and with Perlina and her infant daughter following along in a horse-drawn buggy, they drove a herd of 600 cows and calves 120 miles southwest to Gaines County. The journey took nine days, three of which brought rain, and the family camped out at night.

The unnamed author of the Curry family biography in *The Gaines County Story* had this comment about the trip: "For those in this area who know Mrs. Curry, to see the decorous and immaculate lady—the epitome of gentility—riding night guard on a trail drive is hard to imagine."

In Gaines County the Sherman children attended school at Sawyer Flat, a one-room schoolhouse some thirty miles east of the newly organized town of Seminole. The school offered only the first eight grades, and Mabel, seventeen at the time, found herself trapped on the ranch.

She spent several unhappy years, helping her mother with the endless chores of providing food, clothing, and shelter for a large family, and tutoring her younger brothers and sisters. Then in 1910 Mr. and Mrs. Sherman decided to send her to Sisters of Mercy Academy in Stanton for some higher education.

In 1882 the Catholic Church had dispatched a group of Carmelite Fathers to establish a monastery and convent along the tracks of the Texas and Pacific Railroad, to serve the religious needs of a sparse but growing population in the vast region between Ft. Worth and El Paso. They chose Stanton, in Martin County, sixty miles west of Colorado City, as the location for the original structures, which were built of adobe on a hill overlooking the town from the north.

In 1897 the Carmelite Fathers left the property and sold it to the Sisters of Mercy, an order of nuns from San Francisco, California. As a way of supporting themselves, the sisters opened a boarding school and offered young people in West Texas their only opportunity to pursue a higher education.

By the time Grandmother attended Mercy Academy, it had an enrollment of 100, mostly girls, and most of them daughters of ranchers from Big Spring, Midland, Odessa, San Angelo, Menard, Lubbock, and Post. They studied literature, Latin, rhetoric, needlework, and music, and if Grandmother was an example of what the sisters turned out at Mercy Academy, they were excellent teachers.

When she returned to the Sherman ranch, her future looked bleak. Joe Sherman expected her to teach at Sawyer Flat School, but Mabel had other things in mind. When Buck Curry proposed marriage, she accepted.

They were married in 1912 and Joe Sherman refused to attend the ceremony. As my mother put it, "He felt he needed to ride pastures that day." He was so bitter against the union that he disinherited Mabel and didn't speak to her for two years.

I gather that the Shermans admired some qualities in Buck Curry. He was a hard worker, resourceful, and intelligent. He had come to Gaines County in 1905 from Buckholts, probably to escape the chronic sinus problems he had suffered as a boy in Milam County. Like Joe Sherman, he had only a third grade education, yet on his own he had read deeply in history, law, engineering, and mathematics.

What they didn't like about Curry was that he was loud and flamboyant. The Shermans tended to be quiet, self-effacing people, much like the Quakers of Estacado, and they found it hard to give their daughter to a man who went around dressed in white linen suits and a coyote skin coat.

The Gaines County history book records these observations about Buck Curry: "He held forth in the old red bank building on the south side of the square where there was a monstrous stuffed rattlesnake in the window. When he laughed his booming and hearty laugh, people all around the square smiled, and when he sneezed, it was a terror."

Buck Curry did well for himself. At one time he was general manager of a 64,000 acre ranch owned by a doctor in New York. The ranch employed up to thirty cowboys and ran 2500 head of cattle. By the time he died in 1947, he had acquired a ranch of his own northwest of Seminole.

My grandmother moved into the house at 209 Avenue E Northeast as a bride in 1912, and she was still living there in 1973 when she died at the age of eighty-four—to her last day a beautiful and dignified lady.

When the family gathered for the funeral, one of our tasks was to dispose of the articles she and Buck had accumulated over a lifetime, including a library with three walls lined floor-to-ceiling with books.

These thousands of books reflected the interests and curiosity of Buck and Mabel: histories of Texas, New Mexico, the Civil War, the Jews, the Greeks, the Egyptians, and Indians of the Southwest; books on law, ethnology, soil conservation, and ranch management; books on engineering, wildlife, taxidermy, poetry, china painting, needlework, and biblical studies; biographies of generals, presidents, outlaws, lawmen, explorers, and the framers of the U.S. Constitution; and Grandmother's textbooks from Mercy Academy, with her "Mabel Sherman, 1910" written in a neat hand in the front of each one.

The Underhills, Shermans, and Currys moved to the Texas frontier to find something, to build something, to preserve something they considered important. They did that and now it belongs to those of us who follow.

History tells us that the Quaker experiment at Estacado ended in failure, as by 1890 the last of them had moved on to other places—Lubbock and Wichita, Kansas; and the town of Friendswood, which they established on the Texas Gulf coast.

But those Quakers certainly left their mark on my family. We have all retained their reverence for books. In fact, some of us are even writing books.

I sometimes wonder if the Underhills of Estacado would have enjoyed Hank the Cowdog. It's hard to say. They were a pretty serious lot, those Quakers.

But I know Grandmother Curry would have loved old Hank, and I'm sure she would have recognized at once the spring from which that flow of stories began: those Quakers who came to West Texas in 1880 with their precious books.

The Texas
Panhandle

1984

IN 1820 MAJOR STEPHEN H. Long led the first American map-making expedition into the vast expanse of prairie that lay between the Rockie Mountains and the hundredth meridian.

On August 13, as his party was passing down the Canadian River valley in what is now the Texas Panhandle, they recorded an afternoon temperature of 105 degrees. A few days later they were caught in a violent thunderstorm and pelted with hailstones one inch in diameter. Since there were no trees or shelter on the prairie, they wrapped themselves in blankets and took their lumps.

On August 18, as the expedition moved eastward out of the Panhandle, Major Long scrawled the words, "GREAT AMERICAN DESERT" on his map and gave this assessment of the country he had seen: "It is almost wholly unfit for civilization."

I grew up in the Panhandle and have spent a good part of my life here, and I must admit that at various times I have shared Major Long's opinion of the place.

There is a harshness about it. We don't have quaint rock houses in quaint little towns. We have no shade-giving oak trees. Our rivers aren't very pretty. Sometimes they don't even run water, which is annoying. Our weather is legendary.

In many respects we seem hardly even Texan. We have no bluebonnets and few armadillos. Our winters resemble those in Alberta more than those in Houston. My hometown of Perryton is closer to the capitals of Oklahoma, Kansas, Nebraska, New Mexico, Colorado, and Arkansas than to our own state capital. We are no farther from Chicago, Minneapolis, and

Yellowstone National Park than from Brownsville.

Nor did the Panhandle figure into the early history of Texas. Fifty years after Stephen F. Austin established the first Anglo colony in Texas in 1821, the Panhandle still belonged to the Comanches and Kiowas. While Texans downstate were fighting for their independence from Mexico, debating statehood, sending troops to the Confederate cause, gathering herds of Longhorn steers out of South Texas brush, building towns and railroads and legends, the Panhandle remained just as Major Long had observed it in 1820.

In 1887, the year Edwin Booth gave his first performance of *Hamlet* on the Dallas stage, the town of Canadian, one of the oldest communities in the Panhandle, was being staked out at the mouth of Red Deer Creek. In 1900 the population of Galveston exceeded the population of the entire Panhandle, and the number of lives lost in the hurricane of that year exceeded the number of people living in the five most populous Panhandle counties.

The Panhandle was slow to attract settlers. Better land could be had downstate, friendlier land with wood and water and building stone. Until the Plains Indians were subdued in the Red River Wars of 1874–75 and placed on reservations in Indian Territory, the country wasn't safe even for travelers, much less for settlers with women and children.

As a result, the history of the Panhandle up to 1876 consisted of the diaries of early explorers, the memoirs of a few buffalo hunters, and the campaign logs of the frontier army.

Panhandle history really began in 1876, the year the rest of the nation was celebrating its centennial. That year, Charles Goodnight drove a herd of Longhorn cattle into Palo Duro Canyon and established the first ranch in the Panhandle.

Some historians award this honor to Thomas Bugbee, who set up a ranch in Hutchinson County that same year, or to A. J. Springer, who settled in eastern Hemphill County in 1875. But Goodnight cut such a swath through Panhandle history and left such an indelible stamp on the region that it doesn't really matter that Springer beat him here by a full year. The honor goes to Goodnight, and it should.

Charles Goodnight was the father of our history, and he was a man of exceptional ability and many talents. He lived during a period that produced men of stature, but he towered over all of them. During his long life he excelled as a horseman, cowboy, scout, trail driver, explorer, rancher, and amateur scientist.

He was a man of action, yet he also possessed qualities of mind and spirit that lifted him above others of his generation and put him in the company of Sam Houston and Stephen Austin. It would be no exaggeration to go a step further and say that he was one of the great Americans of the nineteenth century. To find his equal, one would have to compare him to Lincoln, Jefferson, Edison, Emerson, and Twain.

Goodnight saw the obvious but also saw beyond it. In his later years he became something of a legend and was recognized as a frontier hero. He enjoyed his fame but he could also say to the many writers who came to his door, "It's a nuisance to be a frontiersman." Toward the end of his life, his second wife insisted that he embrace the Christian faith, a move he had always resisted. At the age of ninety-three he was baptized in a stock tank near Happy, Texas. When someone asked to what church he belonged, he replied, "I don't know, but it's a damned good one."

By the time Goodnight entered the Panhandle on a Bronze Age tool— the horse—the rest of the nation had already entered the Industrial Age. The Panhandle strolled into the twentieth century without history or tradition. While East Texas had its ties with the Old South and the Civil War, South Texas its ties with Mexico, and Central Texas its strong tradition as the cradle of Texas Independence, the Panhandle began as a historical orphan.

The only parent it ever had or knew was the Industrial Revolution. Had it not been for three artifacts of the Industrial Revolution—railroads, barbed wire, and windmills—the region might have remained wild and uninhabitable up to the present day.

Goodnight served as a living bridge between Bronze Age pastoralism and the age of technology. He was a man without roots or strong regional ties, whose ancestors drifted from Pennsylvania to Virginia, North Carolina, Kentucky, Illinois, and then to Texas in 1845. Throughout his life he was an innovator who did not hesitate to use the tools of the industrial era. He was never guided by sentiment, and his eye was on the future, not the past.

Though he had seen the high plains in its natural, wild state and had loved it, no other figure played a larger role in taming it and ushering it into the modern era. The day he rode into Palo Duro Canyon in 1876 marked both the beginning and the end of the Panhandle frontier period—the beginning because Goodnight was among the first to arrive; the end because his restless mind could not allow the country to remain in its wild state.

Goodnight's first action in the Panhandle was to drive the native buffalo out of Palo Duro Canyon, where they had lived for centuries, and replace them with Longhorn cattle. Later, he replaced the Longhorns with higher-bred British cattle. He was among the first ranchers in the Panhandle to drill water wells, erect windmills, and use barbed wire fencing—all modern inventions brought from the industrial East by railroad.

The railroads came into the Panhandle in 1887 and left a mark on the region that persists to this very day in the location of towns. Up until the 1870s towns in Texas and other parts of the nation were staked out in locations that satisfied the two most pressing needs of the population: firewood and drinking water. Hence, we find Austin on the Colorado River, San Antonio on the San Antonio River, Waco on the Brazos, and Dallas on the Trinity.

Panhandle towns were not built along streams or rivers but along the railroad. The Canadian River runs the entire width of the Panhandle, yet today only one town survives along its course—Canadian, Texas—and Canadian has survived in this location because it happens to be on the Santa Fe mainline, not because of its proximity to the river.

Because the railroads preferred to lay their track across flat country, towns which sprang up along the rail lines shared many of the same qualities: few hills, few native trees, and streets that were laid out on the points of a compass.

Outsiders who drive through the region today notice this more than the natives, and probably leave with the impression that all Panhandle towns were stamped out by a machine. They might also leave with the impression that the Panhandle is uniformly flat, treeless, and streamless, which is not quite the case. It just happens that the towns which were built in scenic locations—Plemons, Tascosa, Lipscomb, Hansford, and Ochiltree, to name a few—have vanished, while the towns which built along the railroads—Amarillo, Pampa, Borger, Perryton, Hereford, and Dalhart—have grown and prospered.

Towns tell of their history through architecture. Little towns tucked away in the forests of East Texas evoke the antebellum South. In San Antonio one sees the influence of Mexico. The little towns in the Hill Country still bear the mark of German settlers who entered the region between 1830 and 1850. Driving past the old mansions in Weatherford, one is reminded of the traildrivers and cattle barons who built them.

Panhandle towns reveal a region which is not yet a century old and which had no close ties with the South, Mexico, or even downstate Texas. Most of the buildings were not made of native stone or timber (of which there was little or none) but of lumber and brick which came on railroad cars.

The most striking edifice in a small Panhandle town is not a cathedral or even a courthouse, but the grain elevator, an enormous white skyscraper made of cement and built to hold wheat and milo harvested in surrounding fields.

The elevator is not a monument to God or to the past. It is a machine disguised as a building, in which grain is stored, turned, moved, handled, and loaded into trucks and boxcars. If it is a monument to anything, it is a monument to commerce, thrift, and productivity. And it is a fitting symbol of a region that was spawned by the Industrial Revolution and whose orientation has always tended toward the functional rather than the aesthetic.

Our towns are where they are because this was where people could survive and make a living. If you worked and saved and got along with your neighbors, you could prosper. These attitudes have persisted to the present day, and while the old Protestant virtues have fallen into disrepute in some parts of the country, they are alive and well in the Panhandle.

Sociologists might refer to this as "conservatism," but it is more than a political orientation. It is a basic and perhaps unconscious instinct for survival. It could be that somewhere in the collective unconscious mind of flat-landers lurks the fear that when hard work, thrift, and individual accountability lose their force, the Panhandle will overwhelm its people.

When Texans talk about the beauty of their state, they don't often mention the Panhandle. We have no beaches, no forests, few hills, no scenic watercourses to compare with the Guadalupe or the Colorado. Ours is not an obvious kind of beauty, and it doesn't always adapt to a postcard format.

Yet there is a beauty and grandeur to be found in emptiness—in being able to see twenty miles in any direction, to watch the approach of a winter norther or the building of thunderheads in July, and to observe every shade and nuance of a sunset in January.

Natural beauty in the Panhandle is so subtle, so closely tied to openness that we sometimes find the richer, more obvious beauty of downstate regions cloying—too rich, too sweet, too cluttered with . . . well, with beauty.

It is risky to generalize and speak of regional temperament, yet on the basis of such generalizations people often make the most important decisions of their lives. To many of us who grew up here on the baldies, left home, tried out other parts of the country, and then returned to the Panhandle to make homes of our own, what is most beautiful about the region is the strength of the people.

It is hard to say how others perceive us, but I think we perceive ourselves as resourceful, independent, generally fair and honest in our dealings, open to change, self-motivated, and willing to take risks.

These were the spiritual qualities our ancestors brought to the Panhandle, the qualities that enabled them to endure isolation and hostile conditions. When Major Long pronounced the Panhandle "unfit for human civilization," he was reacting against a stark landscape and brutal storms.

What he failed to take into account was the vitality of the human spirit, which not only has the ability to triumph over adversity, but also to nurture civilization in some very unlikely places.

Panhandle
Weather

1984

NATURE IN THE TEXAS Panhandle has a harsh, unforgiving aspect that is expressed in violent storms, howling winds, and a winter starkness that evokes feelings of loneliness.

When I was a child we lived in an old two-story house on Amherst Street in Perryton. In 1948, when I was five years old, I occupied a room on the second floor. I remember the wind howling through the elm trees outside and rattling the old wood frame windows.

The house wasn't insulated and in the dead of winter my room got so cold that I could see the breath in front of my face. Mother piled twenty-five or thirty pounds of quilts on my bed and I learned to stay warm by sleeping with my head under the covers—a habit I have retained to this very day.

There was nothing friendly about that winter wind. It frightened me. It spoke of some terrible loneliness that I could feel but couldn't comprehend. When I began to learn about God in the Baptist Sunday school, it didn't surprise me that He had a wrathful side.

Growing up, I saw the storm god many times. In 1955 the Panhandle lay in the grasp of a terrible drouth. The pastures were grubbed down to the roots and the fields were parched and bare. In the spring of that year we were thrashed by winds that brought terrible dust storms.

I remember the first one I ever saw. Nothing in my experience had prepared me for that sight. Off to the north, a black wall moved toward us across the prairie. I would guess it reached a full mile into the air. I had grown up in a church where the preachers often spoke of the Last Days, and I assumed this was IT. I was terrified.

A couple of years later we had the blizzard of 1957. It snowed for two days and nights, and a stiff north wind piled up drifts that buried cars, fences, highways, and even some houses.

For days after the storm you could step outside and never hear the drone of a motor. The entire Panhandle was buried. Air Force helicopters out of Amarillo dropped food and supplies to ranch families and men stranded on drilling rigs.

The husband of Mrs. O'Brien, who lived behind us, was stranded on a drilling rig for a week, and she was left alone to take care of her three small boys, with the wind howling outside, the telephone dead, and the electricity out all over town.

A lot of cattle died in that storm. They didn't freeze to death, they suffocated. They would drift with the wind until they came to a windbreak or shelter. As they crowded toward the warmth and protection at the center, animals were knocked down and trampled. I saw a windbreak south of town where fifty steers had died this way, in stacks and layers.

It was a terrible storm for cattlemen, but for us kids it brought an unexpected holiday from school. Town kids stayed out of school a week, and some of the country kids didn't make it to town for several weeks. I remember that some of my pals and I made snowshoes of plywood and walked from one back yard to another on snowdrifts that had buried the five-foot fences.

In the summer of 1957 we got another pounding from the elements. One hot afternoon in August, a big green cloud appeared in the north. The air became as still as death and the hail came, big chunks of ice the size of golf balls, then the size of oranges.

The streets were flooded, and those orange-sized hailstones looked like cannonballs when they hit the water. Perryton was beaten to a pulp. Our house on Amherst had five windows on the north, and all five were knocked out within minutes. My mother and sister, who were alone in the house, dodged ricocheting hailstones and flying glass, hung blankets over the windows to keep out the rain, and somehow managed to move my father's Baldwin grand piano out of danger.

I was sitting in a car with a friend when the storm hit. The roar of the hail on the metal roof was so loud we could hardly hear each other, even when we shouted. We feared for our lives because we thought the hail would penetrate the roof.

One afternoon in June 1962, a cluster of tornadoes went through the southern part of Ochiltree County. With uncanny accuracy, or perhaps through sheer numbers, they destroyed virtually every farm house in an area ten miles wide.

Two of my classmates were involved in the storm. Ann Yates belonged to the class of 1962 and had all her graduation gifts in the family home south of Perryton. The family was warned by a passing motorist that a tornado was coming and they all escaped. But they lost everything, including Ann's graduation gifts.

The next day I joined a crew that went into the storm area to clean up. We went to the Yates place and found that the storm had left nothing but a foundation, a dead turkey, and a trail of sticks leading off to the northeast.

Danny Tarbox and his parents, who lived west of the Yates place, took refuge in a closet when they heard the tornado coming. It struck the house and took the roof. Danny saw his father rising in the air and grabbed him by the ankles. They all survived, unhurt.

Anyone who was involved in the cattle business will remember the winter of 1972–73. I certainly do. On November 17, John Ellzey and I gathered cattle in a snowstorm. That was the first of almost daily snows that went on until New Years.

Wheat pasture cattle were bogging mud up to their hocks and they died by the thousands. The "dead" trucks from the rendering plant in Amarillo couldn't keep up with the supply and dead stock lay in the ditches for months.

Cattle prices had gotten pretty high that fall and a lot of town folks had gotten into the business as weekend ranchers. A month and a half of snow, mud, cold rain, sleet, moving cattle, hauling hay, and dragging the deads to the ditches took a lot of the romance out of the steer business. Weather in the Panhandle isn't always bad. We have pretty days, and local chambers of commerce are quick to point out that our pretty days outnumber our bad ones. But because we"re so far north, closer to Denver than to Austin, and because we're in a windy region, our weather tends to be violent, and changes rapidly.

I remember one Thanksgiving when a friend from Ft. Worth came up to visit. I told him to bring some warm clothes, just in case the weather turned bad. So he brought a raincoat. When he arrived in the Panhandle, the temperature was in the seventies. Twenty-four hours later it was snowing at thirteen degrees, with a wind-chill factor of something like thirty below zero. To stay alive, he had to dress in my winter clothes, which were four or five sizes too large for him, and spent the entire holiday looking like a refugee.

If you live in the Panhandle for a while, you see the angry side of Mother Nature, and you know that she is not always the giver of life. Sometimes she can be a witch with a capital B.

The Canadian
River

1993

I WAS A JUNIOR in high school when I ventured out of the Panhandle and saw downstate Texas for the first time. I saw many impressive sights, but one that struck me especially hard was that downstate rivers had water in them.

Someone raised in South or East Texas would smile at that and reply, "What did you expect? Rivers are supposed to run water. That's what they do for a living." Well, maybe they do downstate, but up here on the High and Lonesome, a river might run a little water, and then again, it might be as dry as a sugar bowl.

Consider the Canadian which cuts through the Panhandle some thirty miles south of my hometown of Perryton. When you approach the Canadian from the north, you drive through mile after mile of flat-to-rolling country—good farmland and good tight buffalo grass pasture land.

Then off to the left you suddenly see a crack in the earth and look down into the depths of Sourdough Canyon. Off to the right the flats suddenly fall away and you find yourself gazing out into a vast panorama: there's Battleship Rock in the foreground, a line of purple mesas behind it, and beyond them both, some five miles away, a ribbon of cottonwood trees.

Now, this is obviously something special. Nature has gone to a lot of trouble to carve out this big trench in the earth. As you drive off the caprock and continue south, your expectations rise and you prepare yourself for something big at the bottom of the hill. You drive five miles through rolling prairie country and come to a mile-long bridge.

You get on the bridge and look down, waiting to see the watercourse that created this magnificent valley. It's almost hidden in the salt grass and tamaracks, but you manage to catch a glimpse of it as you speed past.

That is the Canadian River? That shallow stream of water, maybe ten inches deep and twenty feet across? Downstate, they wouldn't even call it a river!

Viewed in this way, the Canadian River must qualify as one of the major anti-climaxes in Texas. As a river, it's something of a flop. In most places, it would barely float a canoe.

But in fairness to the Canadian, we must say that it wasn't always so tame. The memoirs of pioneers and traildrivers tell of the days before Sanford Dam (completed in 1965) shut off the head rises and impounded the waters in Lake Meredith. Those old-timers saw the river when it was a mile wide, lapping at the tracks of the railroad bridge at Canadian, sweeping everything before it toward the Arkansas River in Eastern Oklahoma, then to the Mississippi, and ultimately to the Gulf of Mexico.

Those who saw the Canadian on a rampage, swam cattle across it and bogged horses in its quicksand, feared it. Today, we don't fear it. The teenagers who race dunebuggies and motorcycles down the riverbed have no sense of what this river used to be. But before the engineers tamed it, the Canadian could be awesome. That's where the wide valley came from.

That valley was home to prehistoric peoples long before the first Europeans saw it. Archeologists have found ruins of apartment villages in several locations along the river, and I have talked with ranchers and cowboys who know of other locations that have never been explored, and who are content to leave it that way.

This sedentary culture, known variously as "Panhandle Pueblo," "Antelope Creek Focus," "Plains Village," and "Panhandle Aspect," irrigated crops and built a vast network of rock villages between 1000 A.D. and 1450 A.D., yet their cities were abandoned and lay in ruins when Coronado passed through the region in 1541—abandoned to the wind and the rain for reasons unknown. Maybe drought, maybe disease, maybe some catastrophic event that has been lost in time.

Yet even these prehistoric farmers were not the first to live in the Canadian Valley. Flint mined from the Alibates quarries, west of Borger, has been found at sites thought to be 10,000 to 25,000 years old. These ancient peoples, whoever they were, fashioned graceful points for their spears from the Alibates flint, with which they killed large game animals, including the mammoth.

Such discoveries make even the Kiowas and Comanches, sometimes regarded as the original owners of the High Plains, relative newcomers, and indeed they were. Both tribes migrated south from the Rockie Mountains and didn't arrive on the Southern Plains until about 1700, 160 years after Coronado had passed through the region and had introduced the horse to the New World.

The Kiowas and Comanches took the horse and made it into a tool of warfare. For more than two centuries they ruled a broad area, striking as far north as Kansas and as far south as Mexico, and leaving a path of destruction wherever they went.

The hegemony of the Plains Indians in the Panhandle was not seriously tested until the winter of 1864, when the federal government in Washington ordered Kit Carson to march from Cimarron, New Mexico, into Texas, where the Plains tribes were thought to be in winter camps along the Canadian River. The Indians had been terrorizing settlements in Kansas and below the Red River in Texas, and Carson's orders were to deliver them a punishing blow.

On November 24, Carson's army of 400 men attacked a village along the Canadian, in what is now Hutchinson County, and were counterattacked by more than a thousand warriors from four Plains tribes. This skirmish, called the First Battle of Adobe Walls, would have ended with the destruction of Carson's army had their retreat not been covered by fire from two mountain howitzers.

The Second Battle of Adobe Walls, which is better known than the First, occurred ten years later, when seven hundred Kiowas, Comanches, Arapahoes, and Cheyennes attacked a small but well-armed group of buffalo hunters at the compound of Adobe Walls. Fighting on the side of the hunters were army scout Billy Dixon, who later received the Congressional Medal of Honor for his part in the Battle of Buffalo Wallow, and Bat Masterson, who went on to gain a national reputation as a journalist in New York. The Indians were led by Quanah Parker, the last great war chief of the Comanches.

Although the siege of Adobe Walls lasted for three days, neither side suffered heavy losses, and to that extent the Second Battle of Adobe Walls produced more smoke than fire—also Billy Dixon's celebrated shot with a Sharps .50, when he dropped an Indian at 1538 yards. Yet the battle dealt the Indians a serious psychological blow and proved to be a sign that the balance of power on the plains had shifted.

The military conquest of the Indians in the Panhandle began two months after the Adobe Walls skirmish, in August 1874, and ended in the spring of 1875. In that period of six months, the Plains Indians who had ruled the Panhandle for two hundred years were conquered and driven to reservations in Indian Territory.

Settlement of the High Plains region began shortly after the conclusion of the Indian Wars. Popular history holds that Charles Goodnight became the first resident of the Panhandle when he drove a herd of Longhorn cattle into Palo Duro Canyon in 1876. Actually, a fellow named A. J. Springer moved three hundred cattle down to the Canadian River a full year before Goodnight arrived, and set up a trading post and stockade on Boggy Creek, near what is now Lake Marvin, seven miles east of Canadian.

Springer's Ranch, as the place was called, was located on the military trail between Ft. Elliott, Texas, and Ft. Supply, Oklahoma, and Springer sold goods, including whiskey, to soldiers going up and down the trail. In 1878 he got into a card game with some black troopers of Ft. Elliott's Tenth Cavalry. The troopers lost heavily to Springer. They accused him of running a crooked game. Tempers flared, words flew, and guns came out. When the smoke cleared, Springer and his cowboy, Tom Ledbetter, lay dead.

So, while Charles Goodnight is remembered as the Panhandle's first rancher, A. J. Springer lies beneath a granite marker in the front yard of Tom Conatser's ranch house. Moral: If you want your place in history, don't get yourself killed over a dumb card game. Do as Goodnight did— live to a ripe old age and make sure the historians hear your side of the story.

Between 1877 and 1881 many of the big old-time ranches established their brands along the Canadian River: LIT, LX, LS, Frying Pan, XIT, Turkey

Track, Laurel Leaf, and Bar CC. Tascosa became the trade center for the ranches in the western Panhandle, grew to a population of six hundred, and acquired the name "Cowboy Capital of the Plains." At its peak, Tascosa had a newspaper, two lumber yards, seven saloons, and a Boot Hill. Tascosa failed as a town when the railroad bypassed it in 1887, and today it is the site of Cal Farley's Boys Ranch.

Oddly enough, there is only one town in the Canadian River valley that survived into the present day—odd because the valley offered the advantages of water, firewood, timber and rock for building, protection from winter storms, and natural beauty. Tascosa, Cheyenne, and Plemons dried up and disappeared. Only Canadian survived—not because of wood, water, natural beauty, etc., but because it lay on the tracks of the Santa Fe Railroad.

Today, Canadian is a thriving community of 4,000, its traditional cowtown economy broadened in recent years by oil and gas discoveries along the river. Built upon a hill overlooking the spot where a modern railroad crosses an ancient watercourse, Canadian embraces both old and new, history and progress.

During a morning's stroll down the steep red-bricked main street, a visitor might encounter Ben Ezzell, the gentle bespectacled editor of *The Canadian Record*, whose thoughtful, progressive editorials have won him the respect of journalists all over the state and made *The Record* a model of the small town weekly newspaper.

Or one might bump into Jim Streeter, a river cowboy since the 1950s. Jim could walk back a hundred years and fit right in with the cowboys who rode line and bog for the old Bar CC and Laurel Leaf ranches. He has the skills of horse and rope that those nineteenth century cowboys admired, and he has something else too—something that's hard to define. Call it dignity or quiet courage or self-sufficiency—the qualities that have accrued to the so-called "myth" of the American cowboy.

Only with Jim Streeter it's not a myth. He lives it every day, whether anyone is watching or not.

They're all part of this river's history—Ben Ezzell, Jim Streeter, Kit Carson, Billy Dixon, Quanah Parker, A. J. Springer, and all the others. They form a stream of stories and characters that tie us to our past and shape what we are.

And, really, this stream of history is what matters and what endures—even if the river doesn't run much water.

Part II

From Buffalo to Cattle

The Texas
Cattle Industry

1983

THERE'S AN OLD JOKE that's been around for years. A Texas cattleman is asked what he would do if someone gave him a million dollars. He thinks about it for a minute, then says, "Well, I guess I'd stay in the cattle business until I ran out of money, and then I'd have to do something else."

That joke is most often told by cattlemen, to cattlemen, and probably the reason it has survived so many tellings is that it contains a hard kernel of truth about man's odd and often frustrating relationship with *bovus Texanus.*

The Texas cattle industry, like most industries, is rooted in economics. The people who went into it after the Civil War were aiming to make money, and most of them did. As J. Frank Dobie pointed out in his classic study, *The Longhorns,* many of the big traildrivers made "barrels of money." But in the next sentence, Dobie adds, "Most of them, however, died broke."

That gives us a clue about the nature of the cattle business. On the one hand, it began as a business enterprise, and it remains so today. On the other hand, it can't be totally explained in economic terms, because ultimately there is something slightly irrational about a way of life that revolves around cattle.

Maybe people go into the cattle business for sound economic reasons. But what keeps them there is something else. Call it romance, adventure, excitement, whatever. It becomes a way of life, and over the years Texans have been inclined to stay with it long after the bottom line said it was time to get out.

Most industries develop around a place which offers a source of raw materials. The Texas cattle industry was no exception, yet it was unique in that its most important raw material had four legs, horns, and a mind of its own. The cow-brute was *alive*. It couldn't be mined, boxed, or stored. It had to be found, first of all, and then persuaded to go in the right direction, and until it reached the ultimate destination, the packing house, it had to eat and drink.

The primary disadvantage of cattle is that they're alive, yet this fact has also given the cattle industry its unique flavor. From the very beginning, it has been a game of wits: will against will, animal cunning against human discipline—and both against the caprice of nature.

The Texas cattle industry began with the Texas Longhorn, a more than worthy adversary in a game of wits. His ancestors came to the New World with Spanish explorers between 1521 and 1540, and by 1565 Francisco de Ibarra reported finding cattle running wild by the thousands.

In his book, *Cowboy Culture*, David Dary notes that there were at least three strains of Spanish cattle brought to the New World: the piebald, the *Retinto*, and the Andalusian fighting bull. These cattle escaped, ran wild, flourished on the abundant grass, and bred as they wished. Over a period of years they began to take on characteristics that resembled their Spanish origins but were also unique to the New World.

Professor Donald Worcester of TCU points out in *The Chisholm Trail* that this process of change was accelerated in Texas during the rebellion against Mexico, when many ranchers were forced to abandon their herds of Anglo cattle, which they had brought from the East. "No doubt it was during this time that the development of the Longhorns began, for they were a mixture of Anglo and native, or Spanish, stock."

The Texas Longhorn became a breed of its own, and Dobie considered the Texas cattle superior to those below the Rio Grande. The Texas breed, he wrote in *The Longhorns*, was "a rangier, mightier-horned and heavier animal than the straight Mexican."

Characteristics of the breed included a wide variety of colors, long legs and tail, high thin shoulders, cat hams, flat ribs, and, of course, the horns which gave him his name. Unlike the British breeds that would eventually replace him, he was not a good converter of feed to beef. By modern standards, he was much too slow in reaching maturity, and did not have the carcass qualities of the blockier, more compact and efficient

British stock. But for the early Texas cattle industry, he was the right animal for the time. He could survive heat, cold, drought, disease, and insects. But best of all, in this age before cattle trucks and railroads, he could walk a thousand miles to market, in effect providing his own transportation, while gaining weight along the way.

Before the Civil War, Texas cattlemen held big cow hunts to gather herds of wild cattle out of the South Texas brush. Often these affairs were held at night when the cattle could be surprised outside of their thorny sanctuaries. After several weeks or even months of this work, the herd was assembled and driven to slaughterhouses on the coast. There the cattle were killed and processed for their hides and tallow, which then moved by ship to ports on the East Coast. The beef was fed to hogs. These hide and tallow factories, called "packeries," lined the Texas coast from Corpus Christi Bay to Galveston Island.

The Texas Coast also did a brisk business in exporting live cattle. The Gulf ports of Indianola and Rockport, both serviced by the Morgan Steamship Line, shipped 40,000 to 50,000 head of cattle per year, most of them to New Orleans. Some even went as far as Cuba.

The Civil War brought drastic changes to the lives of all Texans, and to the livestock industry. The men and boys went off to fight. Herds of cattle were left untended, went back to the wild, and were scattered by winter storms. By the time the men returned home in 1865, things were in shambles. The Texas range was overstocked with thousands of unbranded cattle and the market had fallen to $1 or $2 a head—provided you could find a buyer.

But enterprising Texans soon realized that, while the local market had gone through the floor, there was a strong demand for beef in the North and East. This imbalance of supply and demand ushered in the traildriving period, which is often thought of as the Golden Age of the cowboy.

In 1866, 260,000 Texas Longhorns went up the trail to railheads in Kansas and Missouri, and by 1888 that number had risen into the millions. During the boom years, Texas cattle moved northward in unbroken lines, crossing swollen rivers, passing through Indian country, and following beaten paths whose names would be known to future generations as the Chisholm Trail, Western Trail, and Shawnee Trail.

The traildriving period produced the first generation of Texas cattle barons: George Littlefield, Charles Schreiner, the Blockers, the Slaughters, Dan Waggoner, Charles Goodnight, and Shanghai Pierce, to name a few. These were the men who read the economic signs of the time, furnished the money and brainpower, took risks, and reaped rewards. But the traildriving period did not last long. For a brief moment in history, economic forces bubbling at the core of a new industrial nation had made cattle drives profitable, but those same forces soon brought an end to this colorful era.

Steel workers in the industrial North, who were being fed on Texas beef, turned out rails and spikes and barbed wire. The railroads pushed into Texas, not only providing railheads closer to the source of Texas cattle, but also bringing settlers hungry for land and a new start in life.

By the early 1880s cattle moving up the trail had slowed to a trickle, and by the middle of the decade, the traildriving period had passed into history.

But as one era died, another was born. This was the era of the big ranches, when cattle culture moved northward into the Staked Plains and Panhandle regions. In the decade after the Civil War, this vast area was regarded as uninhabitable—a dry, treeless, wind-swept desert that was good enough for those who claimed it—the fierce Comanches and Kiowas.

But after the Plains tribes were defeated in the Red River War of 1874 and 1875, a few astute cattlemen began to realize that any region that could support millions of buffalo could also provide grazing for millions of cattle. Charles Goodnight led the way in 1876, driving a herd of 1600 Longhorns from Pueblo, Colorado, and established a ranch in Palo Duro Canyon, near present-day Amarillo.

A year later, herds of cattle moved into the Panhandle from all directions and new ranches were established: the LIT, LS, LX, Bar CC, T-Anchor, and others. By the early 1880s, investors in England and Scotland had heard about the unlimited grazing opportunities in the Panhandle, and by 1885 most of the big ranches in that region were backed by British money.

But these investors learned some bitter lessons about the Panhandle. They had heard about the miles of unowned land and the strength of the native grasses, but they had to learn first-hand about the fierce climate. A disastrous blizzard in 1886 left dead cattle stacked three and four deep along a drift fence that had been thrown up across the Panhandle, and the following summer brought a scorching drought. The British got out of the cattle business as soon as possible, took their money back home, and never returned.

The 1880s were transitional years in the Texas cattle industry, as ranchers, both up-state and down-state, absorbed new technology and made the shift from the days of free range and wild cow hunts to the kind of stable livestock breeding operation we know today.

The most important technological development to the rancher, aside from the building of railroads, was the mass production of barbed wire and windmills. Barbed wire made it possible for a rancher to circumscribe his holdings and contain his cattle inside fences. For the first time, he was able to bring in more efficient lines of cattle, exercise control over the breeding of his stock, and conduct experiments in genetic improvement.

Before barbed wire, there had been little incentive for a rancher to invest in improved stock, since his high-priced, high-blooded cow was just as likely to be bred by the neighbor's rannihan bull as not.

The windmill brought other changes. This portable, mass produced, efficient little machine opened up vast regions of arid West Texas to stock grazing by providing permanent water holes where none had existed before.

Americans didn't invent the windmill. Large stationary windmills had been used in Europe and Asia for centuries. What American inventors did was to adapt the machine to American needs, making it small enough to be transported West on flatcars, cheap enough for ranchers to afford, and simple enough for cowboys to maintain.

As the Texas cattle industry moved into the twentieth century, the future of the old Longhorn steer who had walked his way to the Kansas railheads looked dim. The very qualities that had suited him so well to the traildriving period now worked against him. Ranchers were bringing in

British breeds—Herefords, Durhams, and Angus—and experimenting with the Indian Brahman and Brazilian Zebu, strange looking creatures whose natural resistance to heat, insects, and disease suited them to conditions in South Texas.

Texas cattlemen did pioneering work in livestock genetics. At King Ranch on the Gulf, the brothers Kleberg, Richard and Robert, Jr., experimented with the crossing of Brahman and Shorthorn cattle and developed the Santa Gertrudis, the first breed of beef cattle native to the Western Hemisphere. Tom Lasater, a rancher near Falfurrias, combined Brahman, Shorthorn, and Hereford and came up with the Beefmaster breed.

Each of these new breeds had something new and better to offer the commercial stock raiser, and both have gone on to become mainline breeds that can be found on ranches all over the world. (It is even said that the Soviets have herds of Santa Gertrudis, which they shipped out of Cuba after the Castro revolution.)

One of the most interesting developments in the cattle business in recent years has been the revival of interest in the Texas Longhorn. As we have already noted, at the end of the traildriving period the Longhorn fell into disfavor, as ranchers upgraded their herds and bred for a stockier, more compact animal that would convert grass to beef more efficiently.

The old Longhorn suffered such a decline in popularity that he came very close to extinction. It did not occur to anyone during the first half of this century that the Longhorn would ever fit into the modern world.

But the more highly bred cattle carried an intrinsic weakness: the more they were bred for size and a beef-producing carcass, the more difficulty the first-calf heifers had in delivering their calves. Then it occurred to some bright fellow that calving problems didn't exist among the Longhorns, any more than they existed among wild animals. Nature had taken care of the calving problems of the Longhorn through natural selection, and here was a gene pool that seemed ideally suited to solving the calving problems of the over-civilized British breeds.

As a result, the Longhorn breed is making an impressive return from the edge of extinction, and Longhorn bulls are being actively promoted as ideal bulls for first-calf heifers. It now appears that the Texas Longhorn will be with us for a long time, and this can't help but delight every true, down-to-his-boots Texan.

In many ways the Texas cattle industry has changed dramatically in the last hundred years, yet the ultimate objective remains the same: to convert grass into beef, and to make a profit.

The modern cattle business operates on several different levels. The source of all cattle is the cow-calf operation, where mother cows are run on grassland and their offspring are sold as the primary cash crop. The cow-calf operator may have as few as twenty or thirty animals, or as many as five thousand.

Once calves leave the cow-calf ranch, they enter the yearling or stocker end of the business, usually weighing around four hundred pounds. In the late fall and winter, there is a huge migration of yearlings to wheat fields in the Panhandle and South Plains, and to oat fields along the Brazos River. Since wheat and oats remain green in the winter, they provide excellent forage for yearling cattle, and in a good season the gain on a set of steers can amount to two or three pounds per animal per day.

Yearling cattle can also be summered on grass. The gains on grass are not as high as those on wheat and oats, but neither are the risks. Young cattle wintered on wheat pasture are vulnerable to winter storms and sickness, and a wet or snowy season can leave the stocker operator with an unpaid note at the bank and plenty of education.

When stocker cattle reach feeder weight, around seven hundred pounds, they are turned again and enter the final step in the finishing process. Most stocker cattle today go to the feedlot where they receive a finishing ration, mixed by the ton by computer and delivered to the feed bunk by truck.

Before about 1960, most feeder-weight steers and heifers were either slaughtered or shipped to the Midwest corn belt for fattening. But in the years since 1960, the focus of the feeding industry has moved from the Midwest to California, Arizona, and the high plains region of Texas, Oklahoma, and Kansas.

Today, the major cattle-feeding region in the United States is located within a 120-mile radius of Amarillo. This shift was directly related to the rise of irrigated farming in the high plains region, which yields large quantities of feed grains that are the basic ingredient in any cattle-feeding operation.

The Texas cattle industry has come a long way since the days of the wild cow hunts in the *brasada* of South Texas, yet there is at least one theme that has not changed in a hundred and fifty years: it's a risky business and a hard way to make a living.

It is not at all uncommon for a ranch operation with a paper-worth in the millions to go four or five years without showing a profit. With his money tied up in land and equipment, the rancher is a theoretical millionaire who keeps asking himself, "If I'm worth so danged much, why do I have to work so hard and keep going to the banker for money?"

His problem is the problem of American agriculture in general: American farmers and ranchers are too inventive, too productive, and too independent for their own good. And they are operating in a consumer-oriented society that has come to think of a cheap and abundant supply of food as a God-given right.

Sagebrush and cattle don't vote. Urban consumers do, and any time they sense that food prices are cutting too deeply into their budgets, they let their elected representatives know about it. Cattlemen have learned, through bitter experiences under Presidents Nixon, Ford, and Carter, that the federal government will not hesitate to throttle the livestock industry to gain favor with urban voters.

But cow people have always been good survivors. They haven't gone through market crashes, blizzards, droughts, and plagues for nothing. Some will quietly slip out of business, their land going to people with new money: doctors, lawyers, oilmen, and corporations. But most will hang on for another year, another grass season, another calf crop, and another generation of young Texans.

They will stay with it because survival has become a habit, and because fooling around with cattle has always been more than a business. It's a game, a gamble, and a way of life.

Windmills

1980

WINDMILLS HAVE ALWAYS FASCINATED artists and photographers. Maybe their eye is drawn to the vertical thrust of the tower in a country that doesn't have many trees to paint or photograph.

Or it could be that in the windmill they find a story of our life on the prairie—an old wooden tower, weathered and bent by time, its fan thrashed by cruel winds. That stark image can evoke feelings of nostalgia or a shiver of dread.

Yet what could be more expressive of human triumph over adversity than this lonely sentinel on the plains which brings up clear life-sustaining water in a dry and thirsty land? The frontier could hardly find a more appropriate symbol, for the history and settlement of the American Southwest virtually began with the windmill.

We didn't invent the windmill. We merely improved on an ancient concept. Horizontal windmills were grinding grain in Persia as early as the tenth century, and they had been used in Europe for several hundred years before we Americans harnessed wind power in the 1870s and 1880s.

What American inventors did was to apply an ancient principle to a unique American problem, producing a machine that was portable and efficient, and manufacturing it in large quantities at a reasonable price. They did the job so well that the basic design of the windmill has undergone only slight changes in the past hundred years, during which time these wind-driven machines have changed the course and history of the nation.

In Europe the windmill was used primarily to furnish power for flour mills. In ancient villages, the windmill, made of brick, stone, or wood, was a permanent structure with huge arms that measured as much as fifty feet from tip to tip. They were so large, in fact, that the miller's working area was located in the upper level and his lodging often occupied the area below.

When Europeans applied wind power to the movement of water, it wasn't to raise it from underground but to move it from the surface into canals. The classic example of this was the Dutch windmill. In Holland, the problem was not a lack of water but too much of it.

European windmills were equipped with shutters or sails, rather than fixed blades. The shutters could be opened or closed to adjust for wind velocity, while the sails were raised or lowered. In this way the miller could adjust the wind-catching surface of the fan and keep his machinery running at a constant speed.

But what if the wind changed directions? Even though the European mills were huge and permanent structures, they were built on a pivot beam so that the fan, and sometimes the entire lower area, could be turned into the wind. In many instances the energy used to turn the millhouse was generated by a smaller windmill that could be moved about by hand.

For some reason, wind technology didn't transfer immediately from the Old World to the New. A few European-style windmills were built on Long Island in the early 1800s, but their use was not widespread. It could be that by the time America was settled, other forms of energy, such as steam power, had come along, or that the European design was too awkward and permanent to adapt to a people who had their eyes on the western frontier and were constantly moving.

It wasn't until after the Civil War and the opening up of the vast western lands that the need for wind-driven machines arose in the United States. When large cattle operations began moving into the Southwest, they found oceans of strong grass, but very little surface water.

After a rain, the plains might be dotted with thousands of small playa lakes and water holes, making it appear to be a cattleman's paradise. But then it vanished into the thirsty earth after a few weeks of sunshine and dry wind. Even the streams and rivers proved to be an undependable source of water.

The few places that had a constant supply of water were soon settled to capacity, while the upland prairies could be grazed only when surface water was available.

The American version of the windmill responded to this need. Unlike the European mill, which was fixed and immobile, it could be transported long distances by railroad and wagon. Instead of turning ponderous machinery, it performed the lighter chore of raising a column of water from below ground. And unlike the handcrafted European mill, it could be mass-produced.

The American windmill transformed a liability—the searing, moisture-sapping wind of the prairie country—into an asset. Wind became a constant, inexhaustible source of energy that was free and available to everyone.

It is odd that, with the success of the windmill over the past hundred years, Americans haven't done more to develop wind technology. But invention follows need, and by the dawn of the twentieth century, it appeared that American industry would be able to run its machines on oil and natural gas forever. The need for innovation disappeared, and all at once wind as a power source seemed an old fashioned idea.

It wasn't until the Arab Oil Embargo of 1973 that we began to realize that overseas petroleum reserves were not the exclusive property of American industry. When the price of oil leaped by a factor of ten, American inventors began dusting off old ideas and taking a serious look at wind as an alternative source of energy.

Between 1973 and 1983 we did more thinking about windpower than we had done in the previous 150 years. Scientists took the advances made in aircraft and space research and applied them to wind-driven turbines, and during this ten-year period those of us who live in windy country saw something we had never seen before: space-age machines designed to harness the wind.

But then the price of oil plunged back to the $10 level, and the wind turbines that had been erected on the prairie fell into disrepair, before they could be refined and perfected. The crisis which might have concentrated our attention on wind power passed, and once again thinking on that subject has begun to atrophy.

The truth is that modern man doesn't know what he can do with wind power. If steam power, the gasoline engine, and electricity hadn't come along when they did, wind technology might well have advanced to a high level of sophistication. As early as the 1400s, Leonardo da Vinci was drawing sketches of a hot air turbine which was powered by the movement of warm air up a chimney flue, and by the 1700s Europeans were using wind power to drive sawmills, foundries, and small factories.

And if the price of imported oil had remained in the $30–40 range for another ten years, there is no telling what new designs and concepts American inventors might have brought to windmill technology. It's a shame that their work was interrupted. Now it will have to wait until the next oil crisis.

We can only hope that somewhere in shops and garages, a few lonely inventors are continuing their research into ways of harnessing the power of the wind, because regardless of what else we might say about the other forms of energy, wind has one advantage that makes it very attractive. Through two hundred years of history, the Congress of the United States has never figured out a way of levying a tax on it. In this day and age, that's not a bad place to start.

Mr. Barby and
His Buffalo

1976

IN THE FALL OF 1873, Billy Dixon, noted scout and buffalo hunter, established a winter camp on the Cimarron River in Meade County, Kansas, near its confluence with Crooked Creek. "Buffaloes were everywhere," he wrote later in his autobiography, "but like the leaves of the winter forest—disappearing never to return."

Billy Dixon was wrong. The buffalo didn't quite disappear, "never to return." And one of the men who helped bring back the shaggy beast was a rancher in Meade County, Kansas—on Crooked Creek.

I first met Alfred Barby in 1977, when I was cowboying in Beaver County, Oklahoma. Alfred traced his interest in buffalo back to his early childhood. His father, Louis Barby, kept a small herd on his ranch between 1912 and 1920. Of an evening, the huge creatures would hop fences and come up to the corrals, where they would bawl at the milk cows and terrify the Barby children and their mother. The buffalo stayed on the ranch until a severe drouth hit the country. Like everyone else, the Barbys ran out of grass. When the cattle grew so weak from hunger that they could hardly walk, and when the grasshoppers began eating the bark off the fenceposts, the buffalo had to go.

For some forty years, the Barby 76 Ranch was without buffalo. Then, in 1969, when the federal government put some of its buffalo up for sale, Alfred and his brother Rusty attended sales in Garden City and Kingman, Kansas, and returned home with four cows and a bull, which cost between $500 and $1000 each. The next year they added ten heifer calves to the herd.

By 1977 the herd had grown to forty-two head of cows, bulls, calves, and yearlings. They were kept on a quarter-section of bottom land on the

76's Laverne, Oklahoma, ranch, directly north of the Beaver River. The pasture was bounded on the east by Highway 287, and the herd could be seen from the road. There were no signs to call attention to the buffalo, no eight-foot cyclone fences, no park rangers. This was a working cattle ranch, and travelers passing through the country must have wondered what a herd of buffalo was doing out there.

So why *were* they there? Alfred didn't have a practical, bottom-line answer to that question. Why does a man buy a Charlie Russell bronze, an old saddle, a handmade pair of boots? Why does he keep a dozen horses around when he would get by with three?

"They have their place in history," Alfred said. "They were part of the country, and I think it's good that people driving down the highway can look out and see a herd of buffalo."

A sense of history, then, the same instinct that had prompted Charles Goodnight to start his herd of buffalo in 1878—without which the breed might have disappeared.

Buffalo are not cattle, and they must be handled in a special way. Certain rules must be observed.

You don't ride into the herd and try to cut out a single animal. Buffalo have a powerful herd instinct and will not allow themselves to be split up.

Nor do you ever put yourself between a buffalo cow and her calf. They take motherhood seriously.

You don't want to get in the path of one when he decides to move. Where a cow might go around you, a buffalo won't.

And you don't want to get into a horse race with one. They are very fast and quick, and have tremendous endurance. "You can chase one twenty miles," said Alfred, "and he may have his tongue hanging out, but he'll be ready to run some more."

The mixing of bulls can also present a problem. Bull calves can be introduced into the herd, but if an older bull is brought in, he is challenged. According to Alfred Barby, buffalo bull fights aren't the gentlemanly butting affairs that cow-brutes carry on around the feed ground.

The buffalo bulls will fight until the matter is settled. Sometimes the losing bull is whipped off, in which case he leaves the herd and will probably turn up in the neighbor's pasture. Other times it is a battle to the death. Buffalo don't subscribe to the civilized notion that the wounded should be spared. Wounded bulls are killed, which was the fate of the original bull in the Barby herd.

The Barbys didn't have much trouble keeping their buffalo at home. Six barbed wires on steel posts surrounded the pasture. Any ordinary cow could have gone through it if she had wanted to, and the buffalo could have made even easier work of it if they had wanted. But they seemed content to stay home, which confirmed Mr. Barby's theories about how they should be handled.

Working with buffalo in close quarters presents another set of problems. If cornered and provoked to anger, they can be dangerous. Working pens must be modified to hold them. The crowding pen at the Laverne ranch is over eight feet tall. Trucks and trailers used to transport them must be covered, else they will try to jump out.

The Barbys had worked the buffalo through a squeeze chute on two occasions, to vaccinate them for worms. They used a Brahman-sized WW cow chute for calves up to two years of age. The mature cows and bulls, too tall for the chute, were worked in a stout alley made of two-by-eight lumber. Pipes were slipped behind them to hold them in place.

Under the best of circumstances, it is difficult and dangerous work. Not only are the buffalo big and strong (the oldest bull in the herd stood six feet at the hump), but they also have the ability to accelerate from a standing position to a run in a split second. The cowboy crew must be quick to catch them, and quick to stay out of the way. It was not a job Alfred looked forward to doing again.

The Barbys kept their freezers stocked with buffalo meat. They butchered two-year old bulls (they didn't castrate the males) weighing around 1100 pounds, and Mrs. Barby rated the meat "almost as good as beef." It had taken her a while to get used to cooking the grass-fat buffalo. Since the meat was very lean, she added beef tallow to the hamburger. She cooked her roasts longer than a beef roast. She tenderized the T-bones and sirloins and ground the other steaks into hamburger because of their toughness.

As a breed, the buffalo has certain characteristics which, on paper, make it attractive as a commercial meat animal: natural resistance to disease and insects, no calving problems, strong survival instincts, a dressed-carcass percentage of around 50%, and a lifespan of twenty to thirty years. Charles Goodnight claimed that some of his buffalo cows bred back at the age of thirty-five.

Even so, Alfred Barby didn't anticipate that the Hereford cow would be replaced by the buffalo any time soon. He gave two reasons for that.

First, temperament. In captivity, buffalo gentle down but never lose their wild instincts, and that means they must be handled with care. Second, they do not breed back as quickly as a cow, often skipping a year.

In 1977 the Barbys' herd had a fifty percent calf crop, and at that rate it would be hard to produce large quantities of meat at a competitive price. Alfred figured that buffalo meat would remain what it has always been, a novelty dish. In the meantime, the 76 Ranch went on about the business it had been doing since Louis Barby established the brand in 1900, raising good cattle for market.

In 1977 the 76, a partnership between Alfred and Rusty, ran 1700 cows on 36,000 acres. The operation consisted of four ranches spread over three Kansas counties and two in the Oklahoma Panhandle. The Barbys maintained a herd of 200 registered Hereford cows, with the remainder commercial cows, mostly Hereford. They did not crossbreed except on first-calf heifers, when a black Angus bull was used.

The 76 took its calves through the winter on wheat pasture, and at one time they fed out some of their yearlings in several feedlots. "That little hobby," said Alfred, "was even more expensive than raising buffalo."

But perhaps there is a way of making money on buffalo. In 1976 a friend sent Alfred a Neiman-Marcus Christmas catalog. Attached was a note that said, "Turn to page 26." Turning to that page, Alfred discovered that the department store was selling a matched pair of His and Her buffalo calves. Price: $11,750.

Said Alfred, "I ought to write them and offer to sell them a few for half-price."

Part III

The Cowboy

Some Babies Still Grow Up To Be Cowboys

1983

I REMEMBER THAT DAY in March 1980 very clearly. It was one of the worst days of my cowboy career.

Cold rain had been falling for a week, and the entire northern Panhandle had become a mudhole. Tom, my cowboy partner, and I were ahorseback, trying to gather 150 steers off a wheat field east of Perryton.

The temperature hovered around thirty-four degrees, and a razor-sharp northeast wind pushed waves of rain across the prairie country. Our horses staggered through mud that was six inches deep.

My chaps were soaked, my cowboy hat heavy with water, my fingers numb inside soggy leather gloves. Rain dripped off my ears and down the back of my neck. My glasses were so wet and foggy that I could hardly see where I was going.

All at once Tom began singing, and the words of his song expressed our misery about as well as any song could have: "Mammas, don't let your babies grow up to be cowboys!"

I've heard that this line originally appeared in a newspaper back in the 1880s. A modern composer ran into it, wrote a song about it, and Willie Nelson took it to the top of the country-western music charts.

I have an idea that mammas living in Texas in the 1880s didn't encourage their boys to become cowboys. It was a rough and tumble kind of existence: lonely, dangerous, and full of hardship. Yet it drew young men like a magnet.

The cowboy has become the most powerful mythical character in our folklore, one which reaches to the core of our identity as a people. He is known in every corner of the globe, and is often associated with a place called Texas. Just as the figure of Uncle Sam represents America, the cowboy has come to represent the spirit and history of Texas.

Actually, it's not quite correct to speak of *the* cowboy, as though there were only one kind. Over the decades, we Americans have imbued the man on horseback with so many qualities that he has become a whole cast of characters: the singing cowboy, the Hollywood cowboy, the rodeo cowboy, the dime-novel cowboy, and most recently, the urban cowboy.

All these characters draw their mythical strength from the same source, the working cowboy, whose identity took shape during the trail-driving period after the Civil War. He was a laborer, a workingman whose principal tools were a horse and a catch-rope.

He gathered wild Longhorns out of the South Texas brush and drove them across a thousand miles of hostile country to railheads in Kansas. He rode the line for the big, old-time ranches: the XIT, LIT, Bar CC, JA, LS, and the Matador. He slept on the ground or in a line camp shack. He had no family and few possessions. At the end of his useful life, he had no pension and no ranch to retire to, only arthritis and memories of the "honor" of being a cowboy.

If mammas didn't want their babies to grow up to be cowboys, it was for good reason. In many ways cowboying was a lousy job.

But cowboying has always been more than a job. It is a way of life, and today, in the age of space travel, it continues to draw a small number of young men.

The working cowboy has not disappeared. He may be hard to locate and hard to distinguish from the other young bucks who strut around in cowboy clothes, but in little backwater towns all over Texas, he can still be found.

The modern cowboy's work routine, style of dress, and pattern of existence are determined by several factors: weather, terrain, local tradition, and the size of the ranch he works for. In a state as big as Texas, which offers such a wide variety of climate and geography, it is risky to make too many general statements about the "average cowboy." What is average in the Davis Mountains might be unknown in East Texas. Practices that are commonplace in the Panhandle might seem strange down on the Texas Gulf Coast.

In West Texas the weather is dry, and this single fact determines the entire region's approach to cattle raising. Arid conditions translate into short grass and water problems, and the shortage of vegetation demands that pastures and ranches cover a large area. So West Texas is big ranch country. For that reason, it is probably the most "cowboy" of any region in Texas.

The cowboy who wants a rugged life, isolation, and plenty of wide open spaces might want to go to Van Horn or Alpine to apply for a job.

On the other side of the state—sometimes it seems the other side of the world—lies East Texas, where dust and drought are less a problem than mud, dense vegetation, and insects. East Texas is the least "cowboy" of all the regions in Texas. Ranches and pastures tend to be small, and historically and geographically, East Texas is more Southern than Western. Yet East Texas supports a large cattle population and is a major source of stocker calves, and where you find cattle, you find cowboys.

In South Texas the cowboy orders his work routine around heat and brush. In the summer he will probably start his day at first light and try to get most of his heavy work done in the cool of morning, since strenuous labor in humid heat is hard on men, horses, and cattle.

Not all of South Texas is brushy—the coastal plains are as flat and bald as anything you could find in the Panhandle—but large portions of it are covered with dense brush. The *brasada*, about which J. Frank Dobie wrote so much, makes its own laws with thorny vegetation that can hide cattle and tear a man to pieces. South Texas cowboys, often of Mexican extraction, must develop their own special techniques for working in brush.

And then there is the Panhandle, my country. We have no South Texas brush, no East Texas forests, no West Texas mountains and deserts. Our country runs from flat to rolling, and the element of nature which most intrudes into a cowboy's life is the wind.

A hot summer wind will blast the country into brown brittle submission. In the winter a strong north wind can drop the chill factor to forty or fifty degrees below zero and drift snow over the top of a house. Where a cowboy in East or South Texas must adapt his roping techniques to brush and timber, the Panhandle cowboy has to learn how to rope in a high wind, and that includes figuring out how to keep his hat on during the chase.

Now that we have acknowledged the different approaches to cowboying in different parts of the state, let's sketch out an average cowboy in the part of Texas I know best: the "upper left-hand corner."

Joe Cowboy works on a small-to-medium sized, family-owned ranch that covers twelve sections (twelve square miles) of the Panhandle.

We'll say he is thirty years old, married, and has three small children. He and his family live in a mobile home on the ranch, twenty-five miles from the nearest town. In 1985 Joe draws $700 a month cash salary, with house and beef furnished. He provides his own rigging (chaps, ropes, saddles, bridles, spurs, gloves), while the ranch provides horses and a pickup for work.

Joe's workday varies with the season of the year. In the spring and summer he is likely to work twelve hours a day, six days a week, while in the fall and winter, darkness and bad weather will cut his hours down to eight or nine per day. He doesn't watch a clock or aim for a certain number of hours per week. He tends to work until the job is done or until he runs out of daylight.

The type of work he does also varies with the seasons. The summer will find him repairing the ranch's thirty miles of barbed wire fences, checking windmills, putting out stock salt, and "prowling" pastures ahorseback to keep an eye on the cattle.

In the fall he will join with cowboys on neighboring ranches and participate in the fall roundup season, when cattle are gathered and the calf crop is either weaned or shipped off to market. Every morning during the shipping season he will haul his horse in a stock trailer to the assigned pasture. Joe is a modern, motorized cowboy, and hauling his horse thirty or forty miles to a roundup is nothing out of the ordinary.

The cowboys will get their noon meal from the wife of the rancher whose cattle are being worked. She will meet the crew at a predetermined time and place, carrying red beans, potato salad, fried steak, cornbread, cobbler, and iced tea in the back of a four-wheel drive pickup, the modern equivalent of the old-time chuck wagon, which has disappeared from all but a few big ranches. At the end of the day, Joe will trailer his horse back home.

When the Panhandle winter sets in, Joe will dig out his warm clothes—long-john underwear, ski gloves, wool cap, down-filled vest, and insulated snow boots—and begin the winter routine of feeding the cattle, which begins after Thanksgiving and continues until green grass comes.

After loading his pickup with sacks of protein feed, he will drive from pasture to pasture, honking his horn. When the cattle come up, he will count them and string out the feed, then drive on to the next pasture. In open weather, feeding cattle is not particularly hard work, but when the north wind is howling and snow is drifting over the baldies, Joe will earn his wages.

Spring is the time of year Joe likes the best. The days have grown longer and warmer, and the air is filled with the delicious odors of green grass and the blooms of the wild grape and sand-hill plum. But best of all, it is time for the spring roundup season.

Again, Joe will join cowboys from other ranches. The crew of ten to twelve men moves from pasture to pasture, from ranch to ranch, rounding up and branding the spring calves. Joe will have the opportunity to work his young horses, use his roping skills, and visit with other cowboys who, like him, have been cooped up all winter.

They will talk about horses, roping, rodeo, the neighbors, and maybe a scandal or two. They will indulge in their favorite vices (chewing tobacco and dipping snuff) and miss no opportunity to play pranks on each other.

When Joe goes to town, it is usually for a reason—to buy groceries, windmill parts, or horse feed. His life and rhythms revolve around the ranch, and he tends to grow restless in town. He doesn't know many people and there isn't much to do in town but spend money, which he doesn't have.

Hollywood movies of the 1950s created the impression that cowboys were hard drinkers and that their trips to town led inevitably to the saloon. Hollywood cowboys probably *were* hard drinkers, but working cowboys who hold down steady jobs aren't. If they spend too much time with the jug, they lose their jobs.

Joe isn't a saloon man. He'll have beer now and then, or maybe a few bourbons on Saturday night, but he doesn't drink on the job and his consumption of spirits is likely to fall below the national average.

Joe loves his work and takes great pride in it. He's good at it. He savvies cattle, he's patient with horses, and he has spent years developing his roping skills. Now and then he dreams of moving farther west and taking a job on a big ranch in the Big Bend or maybe a mountain ranch in New Mexico—a real cowboy outfit.

But there is a shadow over Joe's dreams. He is thirty now, and he has begun the process which cowboys often refer to as "looking at your hole card." That means looking to the future, measuring his love of cowboying against the wants and needs of his family.

Next year his oldest girl will start school. She will need clothes and lunch money. Joe's wife hasn't had a new dress in two years. The baby has allergies and will need some special (and expensive) medical attention. The family car could fall to pieces any time.

And although Joe is an excellent cowboy, his wages don't cover expenses in a period of rising prices. Seven hundred bucks a month goes fast.

Joe begins to understand that cowboying is a young man's game. Old cowboys tend to be arthritic and crippled up. They have no money saved up, no property, no pension. Cowboying is all they know, and sooner or later their ranches will have to let them go.

Joe must take a cold, hard look at the "honor" of being a cowboy. Yes, there is honor in it: the honor of being your own man and doing a job well. But there is nothing honorable or romantic about what happens to old cowboys. They may be turned out into a world they don't understand, to sweep out pool halls, move in with relatives, or exist on Social Security.

Joe's dilemma is that he is a highly skilled professional in a profession that doesn't pay much—and never has, not since the very beginning. If he wants to stay in cowboying, he will have to accept low pay, hard work, and long hours—and the prospect of leaving nothing for his children but a few exciting stories.

He knows he could go to town and find a job as a truck driver, a welder or pumper in the oil patch, and make twice or three times the money he's making on the ranch. Or maybe he could go into business for himself and start building for the future.

When he looks at his children at night, he thinks, "I'm going to have to make a change." But when he's out ahorseback, with the prairie wind in his face, he thinks, "How could I ever give up this life!"

Maybe he'll stay on the ranch and maybe he won't. He'll put off the decision as long as possible. If he starves out, another young man will be waiting to take his place.

That's the way it's always been, and that's the way it's likely to remain for a long time. Because no matter what mammas tell their babies, a few of them will grow up to be cowboys.

The Cowboy's Life: Changed But Unchanged

1979

MY ALARM CLOCK WENT off at 4:30. I swung my legs over the side of the bed, found my boots and jeans and shirt in the darkness, and tiptoed through the trailer house, taking care not to wake the children.

I dressed and started the coffee, then walked out on the porch. Off in the trees along the Beaver River, wild turkeys and peafowls squabbled back and forth, alerting their own kind that I had stepped into their world.

I filled my chest with air sweetened by the blooms of locust trees, wild grapes and sandhill plums, and overlaid with the indescribable smell of green grass. It was springtime in Beaver County, Oklahoma, and the mere smell of it left me tingling with excitement.

I walked a dark path down to the barn, a path I had memorized long before, and fed my horse two coffee cansful of rolled oats. In the saddle room I lifted the sheet that covered last fall's white tailed buck and carved a couple of nice little breakfast steaks off the haunch. The deer had hung all winter, improving with age, and it was just about gone.

Back at the house I sipped hot coffee, turned on the radio to catch the morning weather report, and cooked up my favorite cowboy breakfast: venison steak fried in butter, and two eggs. Breakfast done, I put on my shotgun chaps, big rowel spurs, leather vest and black felt hat, switched off the lights, left the house in peaceful sleep and walked back down to the barn, enjoying the music of my spurs.

I saddled my horse in a square of light thrown through the open saddleroom door, tied my slicker behind the cantle, and led Little John to the stock trailer, which I had hitched to the pickup the night before. I had learned through bitter experience that hitching up the trailer in the dark was a bad way to start a roundup morning.

Lights on, window down, the radio playing country music from Tulsa, I pointed the four-wheel drive up the hill, rattled across the cattle guard and gathered speed on the wide, sandy road.

Climbing into the sandhills that rolled northward from the valley of the Beaver River, I caught the aroma of sagebrush and saw the first purple glow of daylight on the eastern horizon. It was a good day to be alive. It was a good place to be a cowboy.

We drove north, Little John and I, splitting the springtime air, through the sandhills and into the short grass country that separated the Beaver and Cimarron watersheds, past ranch and farm houses where kitchen windows glowed yellow and showed families preparing for school and work.

Just outside of Knowles, a little Katy Railroad village struggling to survive without the Katy, I eased my pickup off the road and parked in a grassy spot beside four other pickup-trailer rigs. Another pulled in behind me.

I stepped out, stretched my legs and walked over to the red four-wheel drive where the other cowboys had gathered around a thermos of coffee. Hobart and Carl and Kary and Darrell were there from the Open A Ranch; Stanley and Pat and Glen from the Bar B; Jake from the Three Cross; and me from the LD Bar.

We sipped coffee from Styrofoam cups and waited for the red bud of sun to bloom. We talked horses and roping and weather and teased Hobart because he was such a grouch in the morning.

The sun popped over the horizon and began burning away the night mist. "Let's go," someone said. We loaded nine horses into Darrell's big gooseneck trailer, and the six of us who didn't fit into the cab crawled into the back of the pickup.

And off we went to the Cimarron River, that rough country where Fred Tainter had started his ranch in the 1880s and had built an old rock barn. The Tainters were gone now but the barn was still standing, embraced by vines and partly hidden by weeds and trees in a secret valley that had probably not been seen by more than a hundred people in as many years.

Tainters' cowboys saddled their horses by lantern light and lived carefree, bachelor-happy lives there in the valley. By the time I saw the rock barn where they stored their saddles and horse feed, they had all crossed the divide, leaving hardly a trace behind, only the stubborn bois d'arc posts they planted in the ground and the few ancient strands of barbed wire they strung.

I was of a new generation. I carried a nylon rope on my saddle and a plug of cellophane-wrapped tobacco in my chaps pocket. My boots were store-bought, mass produced by the Nocona Boot Co. I had chosen my clothes that morning on the strength of a radio weather forecast compiled by computers in Kansas City.

Our lunch that day did not come out of a chuck box or a Dutch oven, and it was not cooked over mesquite coals. We ate hamburgers prepared at Rosa's Cafe in Gate and brought out to us in a Lincoln car driven by the roundup boss's wife. We washed the hamburgers down with canned soda pop.

When the branding work began, we heated our irons on a propane fire, injected the calves with a vaccine gun made of stainless steel and glass, and that evening we hauled our horses back to our home ranches at fifty miles an hour.

Mr. Tainter's cowboys might have snorted at our new-fangled ways. They would have choked on the news that one of the men who rode with us that day in 1979 is now using a helicopter to find cattle in the tamaracks along the Beaver River.

I imagine they would have judged us soft and spoiled, mere shadows of REAL cowboys. That is often the judgment one generation levels against the next. What is real is what *they* did, and anything that follows and changes is perceived as poor imitation.

Maybe so. Those old guys earned the right to be a little condescending toward those of us who came behind. They were tough. They starved and shivered and sweated and paid a heavy price for their way of life. They were good at what they did, and many of them, had they had the choices we have today, would have excelled as bank officers, engineers, executives, and politicians.

But it also seems a bit unfair to judge today's cowboy by yesterday's standards and to interject that hateful little word, "real." Today's cowboy is as real as he needs to be, real enough to get his job done and earn his wages—which is about all the old-timers were trying to do.

The modern cowboy dresses somewhat differently (probably in better, warmer clothes), has taken on a few new habits (snuff instead of Bull Durham), has adopted a slightly different style of roping (which was perfected in the arena, not on the ranch) and, instead of batching in a covered hole dug into the side of a hill, he is likely to have a family and live in a tenant house or mobile home.

And, yes, his horse spends a lot of time riding in a stock trailer, but that pickup and trailer have increased his range, tripled or quadrupled the amount of country he can look after, and allowed him to do the work formerly done by two or three men.

Cowboys have changed because they've had to change, because the medium in which they live and operate—ranching—is a business enterprise which, like most businesses, either responds to economic forces or disappears. Ranching is the art and science of converting grass into beef. If the American public ever stops eating beef, the cowboy will vanish just as quickly as the fur trapper or the steamboat captain.

That isn't likely to happen any time soon, and maybe it never will, but in the meantime the cowboy must roll with the times and make a few compromises.

I think there is something inside most Americans which makes us want to keep the cowboy as he used to be, since the cowboy, even more than Uncle Sam or the bald eagle, has come to symbolize what we are as a people. The cowboy, in other words, *means* more than he *is*. He has become a repository of our national self-image. He is what we would like to be: strong, courageous, self-sufficient, honest, and hardworking.

Funny, but those were some of the very qualities I admired in the men I worked with in Beaver County in 1979, even though they drove pickups with two-way radios, and some wore baseball caps instead of Stetsons. That makes me think that the cowboy hasn't been corrupted as much as some people might suppose.

And it makes me think that what was most "real," if we must use that word, about the old-time cowboys can still be found on ranches today, wherever men are training young horses and following the cow.

It has to do, not so much with their outward appearance, but in their devotion to a way of life. It's a hard life, just as hard on the women who stay at home in isolated ranch houses as on the men who ride out into the heat and cold. It demands much and offers little in financial reward, but those who are called to it are willing to pay the price.

I can't define exactly what it is that calls a young man into this life or persuades his wife to leave the convenience of town living and go to the wilderness. But it's in me. It comes back every time I return to Beaver County and catch that haunting aroma of sagebrush in the morning air.

I don't cowboy any more. Like many in the profession, I reached the age of thirty-seven, took a hard look at my hole card, and decided that there were other things I wanted to do.

But I admire those who have stayed with it, toughed it out and made it work. And I hope that when they get old enough, my boys will have a chance to ride those old sandhills along the Beaver River and maybe catch a glimpse of old man Tainter's rock barn.

If they do, I bet they'll never forget it. I won't.

Cowboy
Thoughts

1981

I'M IN MY FORTIES now. My old Heiser saddle is hanging by a rope from a rafter in the garage. The spurs my Grampy Buck Curry made on a coal forge back in the Depression years, and which I wore almost every day for eight years, now hang on a coat rack in my office, beside my chaps and two catch ropes and a straw hat that once belonged to Ace Reid's father.

I don't get too many opportunities to use them any more, maybe two or three times a year when I go out and help old friends at roundup time.

I retired from full-time cowboying in July of 1981 but the instincts remain. I still read the "Help Wanted" ads in the *Livestock Weekly* every Saturday afternoon. I still study the condition of the grass when I drive down the highway, and when cattle are grazing close to the road, I find myself checking their ears and eyes and looking for sick ones.

It's hard for me to drive past a group of horses without going into the ditch, because my gaze lingers on them. I can see at a glance that most of them are idle and need riding, and I think to myself, "Boys, it's too bad we can't get together, because I've got the same problem. We'd both be better with more riding."

And when I happen upon a group of cowboys riding close to the highway, their hats pulled down to the tops of their ears, the collars of their coats turned up, their breath making fog in the air, their horses dancing and bursting with energy, I have to slow down and pull over to the side of the road and watch them for a few minutes, remembering when I was one of them.

I have been many things in my life: a farmhand, a bartender, a chaplain's assistant in a Boston hospital, a university student, a village handyman, and an author. But I was never prouder of who I was and what I did than when I made my living as a ranch cowboy.

When you use the term "cowboy" these days, you have to be careful. It's gotten a lot of mileage in recent years. We've had Hollywood cowboys and rodeo cowboys, rhinestone cowboys and Coca-cola cowboys, urban cowboys and midnight cowboys, Marlboro cowboys and Dallas Cowboys.

The cowboy I'm talking about is the ranch cowboy, the guy who makes his living taking care of cattle. Some people think he became extinct forty or fifty years ago, but he didn't. He's still around on ranches from Florida to California, from Canada to Mexico.

The cowboy has been defined as "a hired hand on horseback" and as "merely folks, just a plain everyday bowlegged human." Those definitions are pretty good, although the second one is slightly dated. Fifty years ago, most cowboys might have been bowlegged but today they're not. Why? Better nutrition and less time spent in the saddle, I would guess.

My own definition, if I were pressed to give one, would be that a cowboy is a common laborer with heroic tendencies and a sense of humor, who lives with animals.

There are four parts to that definition. Let's take them one at a time.

The cowboy is a common laborer. There may be some confusion in the public's mind about the difference between a cowboy and a rancher. Even though they often wear the same brand of clothes and drink from the same cup and look just about the same from a distance, they're not the same. They're quite different, in fact.

A rancher owns grassland upon which livestock graze, and he provides the management for the ranching operation. He makes the decisions on when to buy and sell. He hires employees and signs the paychecks. The laborers he hires to care for his livestock are cowboys.

Cowboying is a trade, much like carpentry or plumbing, and those who pursue it for a living have mastered certain skills. Just as you would expect a carpenter to be proficient in his use of the tape measure, level, square, hammer, and saw, so you would expect a cowboy to be a good horseman, windmill mechanic, and fence builder, and at least a fair roper, amateur veterinarian, welder, and stock trailer mechanic.

Cowboys work for ranchers, not vice versa. Some ranchers work beside their cowboys and some don't.

Cowboys usually own very little, often nothing more than a pickup, a few horses, their saddle and rigging and personal possessions. Ranchers own land, livestock, vehicles, equipment, and houses.

Cowboys come and go. Ranchers remain in one spot, and often times are the third, fourth, or fifth generation to live on the ranch.

Ranchers belong to the middle class. Cowboys don't. Theirs is a notoriously low-paid profession which can't support a middle class life-style. They don't really belong to any class. They're just cowboys. They usually associate with other cowboys, are indifferent to politics, and rarely belong to organizations in town.

Ranchers are likely to be married and have a family. Cowboys . . . maybe and maybe not. Cowboying used to be a bachelor profession because ranches lacked the facilities for keeping wives and families. That isn't as true today as it used to be, and many outfits have replaced the bunkhouse, where bachelor cowboys slept together, with a tenant house, which is large enough to accommodate a cowboy and his family.

But being married to a cowboy and living in someone else's tenant house isn't an easy life for a woman, and many a cowboy has had to choose between his job and his marriage. If he chooses to save his marriage, as many young men do, he moves to town and finds a better-paying job. Chances are that his position will be filled by a younger man who is either single or married with pre-school aged children.

"Cowboy," then, is a technical term. To say that you're one is to say that you're qualified to do certain tasks and use certain tools in a professional manner. In its original and strictest sense, cowboying has nothing to do with country-western music, rodeo, movies, saloons, gun fights, dance hall girls, or Marlboro cigarettes.

Cowboys have heroic tendencies. This is probably the most controversial part of the cowboy tradition. There are people in our society who seem to believe that heroes and heroism are a thing of the past, or that heroism never really existed in the first place. In recent years revisionist historians have turned their guns on the cowboy and have tried to do a job on him.

But the heroism of the working cowboy isn't a joke. It isn't a put-on. It isn't something that has been cooked up by an advertising agency, and it isn't something that cheap minds will ever understand.

Cowboys are heroic because they exercise human courage on a daily basis. They live with danger. They take chances. They sweat, they bleed, they burn in the summer and freeze in the winter. They find out how much a mere human can do, and then they do a little more. They reach beyond themselves.

Why does a man who is paid by the month stay up all night with a mare he doesn't own to help her shell out a foal he also won't own, and which might kill him in two years when he climbs on its back for the first time?

Why does a man make the decision to skip his only day off and feed the cattle on Sunday, when he knows the bossman wouldn't do it and that he'll never be rewarded for it?

Why does a man risk his life roping a bull that has gone lame with foot-rot or fight a prairie fire or fix a windmill in a high wind or feed cattle in a blizzard?

The answers to those questions would have been obvious in simpler times: Because the man cares about something other than himself. Because he believes he's a part of a system that's more important than his own comfort. And because it's right to do it and wrong not to do it.

That's heroism on a small scale, and every cowboy I ever knew accepted it as part of his personal philosophy.

The cowboy has a sense of humor. Cowboys belong to one of the few groups in modern America which have retained a strong oral tradition of storytelling. Telling stories has been part of the cowboy's pattern of life from the beginning, and it remains so today.

Cowboys generate good stories because they have stories to tell, based on personal experiences, and because they have managed to preserve the same kind of organic sense of humor that was found in the work of Mark Twain, Joel Chandler Harris, Charlie Chaplin, Laurel and Hardy, Will Rogers, Charlie Russell, and other great humorists of the past.

An "organic" sense of humor draws its inspiration from broad human tendencies and universal themes. It is gentle in tone and its intent is to entertain, perhaps even to teach a lesson, rather than to destroy. That sets it apart from satire and ridicule, whose focus is narrow and whose intent is to inflict damage.

One doesn't often think of a sense of humor being a survival quality, but it is. Cowboys have learned to use their sense of humor as a buffer between themselves and a world that is usually beyond their control, which might include Nature's wrath, animals which don't respond to human reasoning, and a man's own stupid mistakes.

A friend of mine once climbed on a big Thoroughbred mare with a history of bucking. His companion, who was standing nearby, asked, "How long since you rode the old mare?" Before the first cowboy could answer, the mare bogged her head and blew him right out of the stirrups. His head and feet swapped ends and he stuck his nose into the ground. He sat up, shook the vapors out of his head, and said, "About three weeks."

Another fellow was driving back to the ranch late at night. On a country road, he fell asleep and crashed his pickup into a bridge. A bloody mess, he walked to the nearest neighbor's house and banged on the door. The neighbor answered the knock and stared at his friend, whom he could hardly recognize. "My gosh, Joe, what happened!"

"Oh, my pickup quit on me."

One day in 1977 I stopped in to see a cowboy friend on a ranch in Oklahoma. His wife had gone to visit relatives and he had been batching for a week. I asked him how he was getting along.

With a sparkle in his eyes, he said, "Not too bad, but the sink's got so full of dishes, I'm having to pee outside."

The cowboy's sense of humor helps him survive hard times and keep his place in the world in its proper perspective. In the hands of talented people, such as artist Ace Reid and novelist Elmer Kelton, it is also a valuable natural resource that adds softness, humility, wisdom, and laughter to the jagged art forms of the modern age.

The cowboy lives with animals. There was a time when most Americans had some contact with livestock, but in the modern age that has become the exception rather than the rule. Today, most Americans do not see livestock outside of a zoo or participate in the system that brings food to their tables.

The relationship between livestock animals and their keepers is as old as civilization itself. It is a relationship that welds the lives of people and animals together in a common purpose—the survival and well-being of the animals.

It's not the same relationship that a city dweller might have with a poodle or a house cat, and it's hard for people who aren't involved with livestock to understand it. It doesn't involve love or caring in the conventional person-to-person sense, because the cowboy doesn't blur the distinctions between people and animals. To do so would deprive the animal of its identity and function, and make it into a cartoon parody. From the cowboy's perspective, this would diminish both the man and the animal.

If you asked a cowboy if he loved his cattle and horses, he would probably deny it, even though his devotion to them might suggest that he does. He deals with them on a level where respect is the highest compliment. He respects cattle for their size and strength and cunning. He respects his horse for what it can do: its athletic ability, it's vision and sure feet, its intelligence, and its courage.

And although we can't verify this with testimony, I believe that cattle and horses size up a man in exactly the same way and regard him either with respect or a lack of it. And if they don't respect him, he won't last long in the business.

Cowboys spend more time in the company of animals than they do with people. They live on animal time and order their lives by animal schedules. They feed animals and fight animals, help them come into the world and stand beside them when they leave it.

This daily association with animals can't help but effect the way he views himself and the world around him. One result of this is that cowboys sometimes appear to be more successful in their dealings with animals than with people. As the songs on the country music charts suggest, many a cowboy who can read a horse's mind has a terrible time understanding his girlfriend or wife.

Another result, this one more positive, is that animals have a way of improving people—slowing them down, making them more patient, giving them an opportunity to participate in the rhythms of nature. Human beings need the wisdom and companionship of livestock, and animals need the order, discipline, and sense of purpose we bring to them. We are improved through our contact with them, and they with us.

So there is the cowboy as I have known him: a common laborer with heroic tendencies and a sense of humor, who lives with animals.

What about the so-called cowboy myth? Is there any substance to it?

If, by *myth* we mean a kind of legitimate, non-scientific knowledge that can lead us to a deeper understanding of things (as opposed to the common usage: myth = lie), then yes, I say the cowboy myth is not only real, but it's an essential part of who we are as Americans.

We don't have knights or kings or gurus in our tradition, even though we might wish we did. We come from cowboys and that's who we are, for better or for worse. The farther away we get from our cowboy heritage, the less we will know about who we are and how we fit into this vast universe we're still struggling to understand.

I admit that I'm biased, but I don't think it would hurt this nation to hear more about the cowboy and less about crooked politicians, football players, and movie stars.

Several years ago, Willie Nelson recorded a song called "My Heroes Have Always Been Cowboys." Not long ago I was out working with a friend who began cowboying forty years ago. He mentioned that song and said, "You know, that's the way it's been for me. My heroes *have* always been cowboys, and I guess they still are."

I thought about that for a long time. I have two sons, ages thirteen and four, and I worry about the kind of world they're living in. If they decided to make heroes of some of the cowboys I've known, I'd be proud.

The American Cowboy:
Traditional and Modern

1983

TOM AND I WERE cowboys. We worked on a ranch in the northern Texas Panhandle, and to us the coming of spring was a special source of joy.

The winter of 1979–80 had been a bear. The ice and snow and cutting winds of January and February had been bad, but the worst part of the winter had come toward the first of March, with a long period of cold rain. Day after day it had rained. Slow rain, hard rain, rain mixed with snow and sleet, rain driven by a cruel northeast wind.

We had worked out in it every day, wearing yellow slickers and four-buckle overshoes and cowboy hats that were soaked through with water.

But then came spring, soft days heavy with the scent of green grass and the honking of cranes and geese flying north. And, like cowboys everywhere, we were filled with joy.

The coming of spring meant that we could throw our overshoes in a corner of the saddle house, start practicing with our ropes, and get back to working with colts.

Tom had a bay mare named Bonnie that he had been bringing along since the fall. She was a tall, leggy mare, still green and awkward but eager to please. Tom had been patient with her and had brought her on slowly, and she promised to make a dandy saddle mare.

One evening in April we had to drive a herd of steers several miles across country to a pasture along Wolf Creek. It was easy work, just right for a green horse. The sun was slipping toward the horizon when we delivered the steers to the pasture and started back to headquarters. It was one of those times when a cowboy feels that he is one of God's chosen people, a lucky man to have been given the chance to follow the horseback life.

We trotted our horses toward home and played with our ropes, throwing at sagebrush and soapweeds. We came to a steep hill that led down to a draw. I was coiling up my rope and happened to be looking at Tom.

Bonnie stumbled in the caliche rock. She staggered several steps, trying to keep her feet. Her chest hit the ground. I kept thinking she would wallow to her feet.

But she couldn't pull out of it. Her head and neck rolled under. I watched in horror as this thousand pound animal tumbled down the hill and began a forward roll.

Tom was still in the stirrups, with the rope in his hands and a stunned expression on his face. I watched Bonnie's back end go up and over. And as Tom saw what was coming, I heard him murmur, "Oh God."

He plunged face-first to the rocky ground, then disappeared beneath the horse. I had seen wrecks before, but I had never seen one that was so certain to crush and cripple a man as this one.

I dived out of the saddle and ran to him, just as the mare rolled off of him. His eyes were closed, his face compressed in pain. I lifted his head off the rocks and cradled it in my arms. I feared that he might be dying.

"It's all right, Tom. Just lie still."

He blinked his eyes. "I can't tell how bad I'm hurt." He tried to sit up.

"Lie still, don't move."

"Got to." He struggled. I thought maybe he was delirious.

"Don't move, Tom."

"Got to. I'm in an ant den."

I stared at him. *"Ant den!* Son, if you're worried about ants, you're not hurt very bad." I let his head drop.

Five minutes later, we were ahorseback again. Tom walked funny for a couple of weeks, but he was all right. They say that to kill a genuine cowboy, you have to cut off his head and hide it.

I consider myself lucky to have had the chance to live the cowboy life. When I went into full-time cowboying in 1974 I had a feeling that I was getting on the tail-end of an era. When I left cowboying seven and a half years later, I knew others who were going into it with the same thought. They figured this might be the last chance.

People have been building coffins for the American cowboy for about the last hundred years. According to some scholars, he was finished off around 1880 when the railroads brought an end to the traildriving period. Other writers figure the cowboy quit breathing around the turn of the century. Or when the country started getting closed in with barbed wire. Or when the big ranches got split up. Or when pickups and stock trailers came on the scene.

In 1976, *The New Yorker* magazine put out the word that, by George, at last the cowboy was done for. In this "parable of failed promise," it was revealed that the old cowboy had finally succumbed to feedyards and modern technology. And maybe cirrhosis of the liver, since the guy in the story hit the jug pretty hard.

I was cowboying in Beaver County, Oklahoma, at the time *The New Yorker* scooped that story. I was working horseback ten to twelve hours a day at the time, and it was a little hard for me to believe that the American cowboy had been flushed down the toilet of history.

The fact of the matter is that cowboys may be as hard to get rid of as roaches, and for the same reason: they're adaptable. This seems to be an ingredient in the cowboy that writers have missed over the years. It could be that writers, who tend to have a little of the romantic in them, have been drawn to the older cowboys who just naturally look and act and sound more like "real" cowboys are supposed look, act, and sound.

An older man is apt to see change as a corruption. His whole life has been invested in doing things a certain way, and the older he gets the more he begins to think of his habits and patterns as "real," and to regard any kind of change as counterfeit.

I had a great-uncle named Bert Sherman who started cowboying in West Texas around 1920. He worked on big ranches, went out with the wagon in the spring, slept in the snow in a bedroll, and lived alone in line camp shacks. When he was an old man, telling me about his adventures, he always managed to let me know that the days of the "real" cowboy were about gone, and that the young bucks of the modern age didn't know cowboying from Shinola.

If I had been content with Uncle Bert's version of the American cowboy, I never would have gone into cowboying myself. And I never would have learned that Uncle Bert, God rest his soul and bow legs, was wrong.

What he perceived as the end of the Old West and the end of the cowboy was nothing more than the end of Uncle Bert's career. I can't blame him for wanting to take cowboying with him to the grave. It's a natural human tendency, this desire to possess something permanent and dignified, and to pronounce all future activity insignificant.

But it's the obligation of the young not to believe that, and not to allow it. Surely God is wise for making young men stubborn and ignorant, because had he made them even halfway smart, the old men would have been right and the cowboy would have been dead eighty years ago.

Writers who dwell on the death of the cowboy and the end of the West have spent too much time listening to old men. The most important ingredient in the Cowboy Code is survival. Cowboying is alive today because, for a hundred and twenty years, young men have demanded that it stay alive. Through the force of their lives and actions, they have kept it alive, even when it demanded suffering and sacrifice.

This suggests to me that there is a certain spiritual or mythic quality in cowboying that is so powerful, so much a part of what we are as a people, that we will never see the last cowboy. I cannot conceive of any catastrophe that could get him out of our system.

Well, let's take a closer look at the modern cow-chaser and see exactly where and how he has changed. I would say that pickups and stock trailers have changed the cowboy's work habits about as much as anything.

Back in the old days—and I mean up to about 1950 or 1955—when a crew of cowboys went out to do some cattle work, they rode out from headquarters before daylight, walked or trotted their horses to the roundup spot, did their work, and then rode home. On the bigger ranches that had thousands of calves to brand each spring, the crew went out with the chuck wagon and camped, and they might not see headquarters for weeks or even months.

There are still ranches around that use a wagon. In some cases, when the ranch is quite large, this is a necessity and a convenience, but in other cases I would guess that it has less to do with cost effectiveness than with nostalgia—you might call it the evolution of a work-form into an art-form.

But most ranches today don't need or use a wagon. Distances from headquarters to pasture and from ranch to ranch have been shrunk by pickups and stock trailers.

When I cowboyed in the Oklahoma Panhandle in the late 1970s, I swapped out work with neighboring ranches. Every spring and fall, we would throw together a crew of anywhere from seven to twenty-five men. Every morning before daylight, I would load a fresh horse in my stock trailer and drive to the roundup point, meet the crew, do the day's work, and then drive home at night.

Sometimes these were short trips, two or three miles over country roads, but other days I was driving thirty or forty miles to reach the roundup spot. This went on every day for two or three months as we worked our way down the Beaver River and then over into the Cimarron country.

Modern cowboys have been very clever in adapting their work habits to the machine age and putting the pickup-trailer combination to good use out in the pasture. If a cowboy knows the right techniques and has the right kind of trailer, he can use the stock trailer to perform a wide range of jobs.

Let's use one of my experiences as an example. In the winter of 1980 I was working on a ranch in the Texas Panhandle. This outfit consisted of a block of grassland located on Wolf Creek, and in this country we ran mother cows year-round. But in the fall, winter, and early spring, we ran yearlings on leased wheat pasture.

In 1980 we had steers scattered all over the county, about six hundred head on five places up on the flats. These places averaged around twenty miles from headquarters. Since yearling cattle are prone to stray and get sick, they have to be checked closely and on a regular basis.

Usually my partner Tom and I would check the yearlings together, but one day in February I had to do the job alone. That morning I loaded my mare into the stock trailer, threw in a bag of medicine, extra ropes, and a set of come-alongs (that's a small hand-operated winch), and headed for the flats.

At the Wright place, I rode through a bunch of big yearlings and found one that had bloated on the green wheat. If I had come a day later, I would have found him dead. I parked my pickup and trailer in the middle of the wheat field, and left the trailer gates open, which was something I always did. I roped the steer, which weighed around six hundred pounds, and drove him on a loose rope to the trailer.

When I reached the trailer, the gates were already open to receive an animal. I maneuvered the steer around until I could slack my rope and flip it over a steel ball welded to the top of the stock racks. Then I dallied my rope to the horn, spurred my mare, and tried to drag the steer into the trailer.

Why didn't I just drive him to a set of pens and load him there? Because there weren't any permanent corrals, and on wheat pasture there very seldom are.

The steer sulled and went down, and my little mare didn't have enough strength to drag that much weight. So I dismounted, tied the steer down with a pigging string, fitted a horse halter around his head, and winched him into the trailer with the come-alongs. Once I got him inside the trailer, I ran a rubber hose down his throat and let the gas out of his stomach. That gas pressure can become so intense that it will kill the beast by stopping his heart.

With the steer loaded in the front compartment of the trailer and my mare in the back, I drove ten miles to the Bryan place. I jumped out my mare and rode through that bunch and found a heifer with the bloody scours (I apologize for all these unpleasant terms, but they're all part of the cowboy's work).

I roped this heifer, drove her to the trailer, and while the first steer was still shut into the front compartment, I dragged the heifer into the back compartment, closed the back gate of the trailer, opened the center gate, and put both sick animals up front.

Then I loaded my mare in the back and drove seven miles to the Anderson place. I found two small steers in this bunch that just weren't doing any good, so I roped them and loaded them the same way I had loaded the heifer. That gave me four head in the front compartment and my mare in the back.

Then I drove fifteen miles to the Northup Creek pasture. There I found a heifer that was blind with pinkeye. I stuck a loop on her, put her in the trailer, and headed for home.

By the time I got to headquarters, I had covered seventy-five miles, checked six hundred head of yearlings on five different places, and I still had enough daylight to take care of my mare and run the cattle through the doctoring chute.

That gives a pretty fair idea of the tremendous mobility of the modern cowboy, and it also demonstrates the ways one man and one horse can use a stock trailer. It not only hauls a horse around the country, but it can be used as a portable catch pen in remote pastures where corrals don't exist.

Of course there is another way of looking at all this, and it's the way my old Uncle Bert chose to see it. He sneered at the very idea of a cowboy hauling a horse instead of riding him. He saw this as just another example of whippersnappers lowering the standards of the profession, spoiling the horses while tearing up expensive machinery.

The old guys often express their contempt by saying, "There's two things you never see any more: a cowboy riding and horse walking."

Well, that's one way of looking at it, and there's a certain amount of truth in it. There's no denying that the increased use of pickups and trailers has changed the cowboy's relationship with the horse. Obviously, when a cowboy hauls a horse, he's not riding him. Horses today are not ridden as far, as hard, or as often as they were in the old days.

I've heard old-timers say that modern cowhorses are not as skilled as they were when they were ridden ten or twelve hours a day. That might be true, but it's also true that modern horses live longer and work longer for the same reason, because they're not ridden into the ground on a regular basis.

You can argue either side of that question, but there's not much doubt that the modern cowboy doesn't come into contact with the number of horses the old-timer did. The old-timer who went with the wagon caught his horse out of a remuda every morning. A cowboy crew back then might have used a hundred or more horses, and although an individual cowboy might have had only ten horses in his personal string, he had the opportunity to study the habits and dispositions of the entire herd.

In a remuda of horses, he would see every size, color, and disposition, from killers to jugheads, and to that extent the old-time cowboy had a broader knowledge of horses than his modern counterpart.

I think we could come to a similar conclusion about roping. The old-time cowboy had anywhere from six to twenty roping techniques in his repertoire, which might include a regular heading loop, a heeling loop, a horn loop, the Blocker loop, the hoolihan, and three or four loops he used on the ground for roping horses.

A man from Wyoming once told me that he knew an old cowboy who knew twenty different ways of heeling an animal.

It appears to me that the modern cowboy has forgotten much of the old lore of roping. When I was cowboying, I never met a man who knew how to throw a Blocker loop, which was a standard technique up until about forty or fifty years ago, and probably the most versatile loop ever invented. A man who knew how to throw a Blocker could use it for roping heads, horns, forefeet, and heels, which just about covers everything a cowboy would want to catch.

And I knew only a few men who knew how to use the hoolihan, a soft, quiet, counter-clockwise loop that is excellent for roping in a herd.

Most of the cowboys I worked with knew only two loops: a heading loop and a heeling loop. In both cases, the technique came not from a ranching tradition but from the roping arena, where team ropers have developed a fast, efficient style of heading and heeling. These two loops have become the standard roping techniques of the modern cowboy, and ninety percent of his pasture work can be done with them.

The old-time cowboy had a broader range of techniques because he needed them, and when the need disappeared, most of the old roping styles were forgotten.

In both these areas—horses and roping—it would be easy to conclude that the standards of the profession have changed for the worse, and that the modern cowboy is only a pale imitation of his old-time counterpart. If you accept that the cowboy of, say, 1880 was the standard by which all others must be measured; if you believe that the cowboy of that period was the *real* cowboy, then it won't be hard to say that standards have gone to hell and God ain't making real cowboys any more.

My Uncle Bert, wherever he is today, would stand up and applaud that. I expect that Charlie Russell would too, and maybe Mr. Dobie and Ben Green and Spike Van Cleve and a host of others.

I would rather not quarrel with such awesome authority, but I just can't buy that argument. The old-time cowboy did what he had to do to keep his job and earn his wages. He knew more loops and worked with more horses than today's cowboy, but today's cowboy knows more about pick-ups, stock trailers, cattle trucks, livestock genetics, range ecology, animal nutrition, windmill technology, fence building, and veterinary medicine than the old-timer.

And if we wanted to be tacky about it, we could go on to say that the modern cowboy is probably cleaner, smells better, has better teeth and stronger bones, is better informed on world affairs, has a much more realistic view of women (since he's likely to be married to one), is a lot more interested in children (since he's likely to have a few of his own), and doesn't spend nearly as much time with prostitutes as the old-time cowboy did.

If a guy wanted to prove that the modern cowboy is a vast improvement over those dirty old bachelor cowboys, I think he could do it without much effort. But what would it prove? I can't see that we accomplish much by saying that either group is better than the other.

What we can say is that both groups have done what they had to do to keep a job in the cattle business, and over the years they have adapted to changing times. Today's cowboy is not the same as the cowboy of a hundred years ago, any more than today's Quarter Horse is the same as the little cow pony of a century ago. And that's good.

The first duty of any species is to survive. The cowboy has done that, and his mere survival is reason enough to win him respect. What do you suppose the odds are against a man on horseback, a relic of the Bronze Age, surviving in the age of moon landings and computers?

I have an idea that at any point after 1945, the cattle industry could have phased out both cowboys and horses. It could have gone to a completely confined and automated operation supervised by technicians on motorcycles, and if cowboys had made the kind of demands for higher wages and better conditions that organized labor made in the industrial centers, I think it would have happened. And it still can. The technology is available.

Cowboys have survived, not so much because the industry needs them, but because they have needed themselves. They have been willing to sacrifice material comforts and security for the opportunity to participate in a way of life whose roots go back into another era of human history, back to a time when mankind perceived order in the universe, participated in the rhythms of nature, and could believe in the dignity of life, work, and human virtue.

To most citizens of the modern age, that time is gone forever. Picasso must have had this in mind when he painted his famous picture called "Guernica," which shows a horseman and his mount shattered on the ground, like a toy that has been stomped. The painting seems to point to the end of an age when horses and horsemen mattered at all, as if the invention of planes and bombs and tanks had thrust all of mankind into a terrible new age in which the virtues of the cavalier were obsolete, when one dull brute at the controls of an airplane could machine gun a whole regiment of noble horsemen into oblivion, without lifting a saber, dirtying a hand, or even looking his adversary in the eyes.

For a hundred years now writers have been waiting for the cowboy to die, waiting for the message of "Guernica" to reach the American heartland. Yet every year a small number of young Americans makes the decision to take a ranch job. They go into cowboying because there is something in the horseback life that they need and want. I suspect that at least part of what they are looking for is the spiritual quality that has accrued to the cowboy and made him our most enduring mythological character.

The great cycle of history is taking us away from the age of the horse and the cavalier, yet there seems to be something in all of us that doesn't want to give up the cowboy and let him ride into the sunset for the last time.

This makes me think that, just as those young folks who go into cowboying need to keep the cowboy alive, we as a culture and a people need the spiritual vitality of the cowboy in our mythology.

And that's why I don't think we will ever see the last cowboy. We need him. We need to know that he is out there. We need to know that this is who we used to be, and perhaps who we need to be and want to be.

And the more we change, the farther we move out into space and the deeper we probe into the atom, the more we will need him, for he is our magic mirror on the wall. When we look into the mirror, we see our past and our present, what we were and what we have become.

So ride on, cowboy, until somebody cuts off your head and hides it.

Part IV

Cowboy Tools

Saddles:
The Evolution of a Tool

1982

HISTORIES OF SADDLES, SADDLE design, and saddle making have a tendency to get bogged down in technical language, as the author expounds on the mysteries of forks and swells and front jockeys, fenders, billets, horns, gullets, and riggings.

The connoisseur will follow this loving recital of details, while the ordinary mortal stares at the page with glazed eyes and drifts off to sleep.

But it needn't be so technical. The history and evolution of the western saddle is ultimately the story of people and how they used this piece of equipment to improve their lives and work.

The saddle is a tool. The Spanish saddles that Cortez brought to the New World were tools of warfare, the same basic design that had helped the Moors invade and conquer Spain in 711 A.D. This saddle was high in front and had a wrap-around cantle which gave it the appearance of a chair. The stirrups were short by modern standards, in keeping with the Spanish style of riding.

The Spanish war saddle had worked well in the old country. The front was armored to protect the legs of the rider, while the high cantle curved around the rider's back and held him securely in place, even if he was unfortunate enough to get hit by a stray lance. It was often decorated with precious stones and silver, and if it resembled a throne in many ways, that was surely no accident. The Spaniards, after all, were caballeros, gentlemen ahorseback.

The conquistadores were very much aware of the advantages a man on horseback held over a man afoot, and they did their best to keep the Mexican natives on the ground, first by making it against the law for Mexicans to own horses. When that failed, they tried to keep them from acquiring saddles. That also failed.

In the hands of the Mexicans, the saddle of the conquistadores was modified from a war saddle to one that was suited to range work. The short stirrups were lengthened and the high cantle lowered, which made the saddle more comfortable to cowboys who spent long hours horse-back. Then the high fork, which for the Spaniards had been more orna-mental than functional, was made into a saddlehorn—in effect, a por-table snubbing post around which the vaquero could "dally" his rawhide reata.

"Dally" is an English corruption of the Spanish *dale welta*, which meant giving the rope a turn around the saddlehorn. Today's Texas cowboy sub-scribes to one of two methods of roping: the dally method, where a loose rope is wrapped around the horn, or the hard-and-fast method, where the end of the rope is tied solid to the horn.

The dally method, which is used in modern team roping competition, traces back to the roping style used by the vaquero, while the hard-and-fast technique, which is used in calf roping and steer jerking events, was developed by Texas cowboys in the late nineteenth century.

Each style of roping has left its mark on saddle design.

Once the Mexican vaquero had modified the Spanish war saddle, the basic design was in place for all work saddles that would follow. Over the next three hundred years the western stock saddle would undergo many changes in style, but these changes would all be variations on the vaquero theme: long stirrups, lowered cantle, and a horn suited for roping.

Just as the Mexicans had changed the Spanish saddle, so did the Texas cowboys make changes in the Mexican design. Since the Texas boys were doing a lot of heavy roping to capture wild cattle, they strengthed the structure of their saddle by covering the entire tree (the wooden frame) with rawhide, and then covering it on the outside with leather.

By 1860 or thereabouts, many of the Texas boys had gone to shorter ropes made of grass (as opposed to the sixty-to-eighty foot rawhide reatas of the vaqueros) and were tying the home end solid to the horn. This innovation made the big Mexican dally horn unnecessary, and the Texas saddle began to show the narrow horn that marked its owner as a hard-and-fast roper.

And finally, the Texas saddle acquired a second cinch, called the flank cinch, which went under the horse's belly and held the rear of the saddle to the horse's back. This "double-rigging" became the trademark of the Plains cowboy, and today it is a rare saddle that is not equipped with the flank cinch.

The Mexican saddle had only the single rigging in front, and that was all the vaquero needed. He used a long reata and could give slack to a large and snorty animal, much as an angler plays a big fish until he wears him down.

But the Texas boys tied solid to the horn—"If it's worth catchin', it's worth keepin',"they often said—and when a big animal hit the end of the rope, it sent a jerk up to the saddle, causing the back end to fly up. The second rigging held the saddle down and allowed the Texas boys to go on about their business of jerking and tripping down grown stock.

Oddly enough, the appearance of the double-rigged plains saddle created a philosophical quarrel between cowboys of the prairie states and those on the West Coast, the latter fiercely loyal to the vaquero tradition which included the use of the reata, the dally method, and a single-rigged saddle. The boys on the West Coast didn't even want to be called cowboys; they were vaqueros, by George, or at least buckaroos.

In California, it was almost a criminal offense to ride a double-rigged saddle, while in the plains state a cowboy on a "center-fire" saddle would have been laughed out of the country.

Why such strong feelings about a seemingly small detail? In his book *Vaqueros and Buckeroos*, Arnold Rojas, a modern-day vaquero, notes that the vaquero "abhorred the two-cinch or double-rig saddle and despised the man who rode one" because it "inflicted unnecessary pain on the horse." He pronounced the double-rigged saddle brutal and inefficient.

Maybe so and maybe no. You get the impression that this dispute between vaqueros and cowboys had more to do with regional, ethnic, and cultural differences than with concern for horseflesh, and certainly the modern horseman, who votes with his dollars, has given overwhelming approval to the double-rigged saddle.

Even the famous J. M. Capriola Co. of Elko, Nevada, which specializes in equipment for the buckaroo, has gone almost entirely to the double-rigging. Of the forty-two styles of stock saddles shown in their 1985 catalog, only one was single-rigged.

During the traildriving period, which began around 1865 and lasted until about 1880, thousands of Texas cowboys rode the cattle trails up to Kansas, Nebraska, Wyoming, and Montana. They took their saddles with them and many of them stayed, spreading the lore and technology of Texas range life to the northern plains.

As the demand for saddles increased in the north, local saddle makers began turning out their own versions of the cowboy rig. In Cheyenne, Wyoming, Frank Meanea made copies of the Texas "Mother Hubbard" saddle, then gradually added his own modifications, including the "Cheyenne roll" cantle which is a common feature on many modern saddles. In Pueblo, Colorado, S. C. Gallup introduced his version of the plains saddle, which featured an upright metal horn and a high-dish cantle.

The Gallup saddles became so popular that even the Texas boys were taking them home, and by the turn of the century the Gallup was a favorite on the Texas range.

Saddle design continued to change in the twentieth century, but all at once, the changes were coming from a different direction. In the nineteenth century saddles were used primarily by working cowboys, and innovations in saddle design reflected the needs of the working cowhand. But by the second decade of the present century, rodeo had begun to exert a powerful influence in the West, and for the first time ever, ranch cowboys were buying saddles that had been modified by and for arena performers.

It would be hard to overstate the impact of rodeo on the twentieth century cowboy, and any study of the modern cowboy which doesn't take the influence of the arena into account is missing the boat. In our times, the arena has become a kind of laboratory where ideas, techniques, and equipment are tested and modified, then later drift back to ranch country.

This is certainly ironic. Rodeo began as a sport-imitation of ranch work, yet the imitation has become so powerful that it now sets the trends and sends them back to the source. The twentieth century has seen the ranch cowboy imitating his imitator. His ropes, his roping techniques, and the design of his saddle have come from the arena.

The first contest-inspired change in saddle design was the "swell fork" which originated in the Pacific Northwest. The fork or pommel is that part of the saddle which sits in front of the rider, and in the cowboy rigs of the nineteenth century the fork was "slick," made more or less in the shape of an A with the horn sitting on top.

By 1910 saddle makers in the Northwest were building saddles with a swelled fork and a high, dished cantle, which were designed specifically for bronc riding. The swelled fork allowed the rider to suck his legs up into the saddle and give himself a better seat on raunchy horse, and the dished cantle kept him from going out the back end.

The swelled fork found immediate acceptance from contest riders, and the design soon spread to ranch country. Indeed, the swell fork idea seemed so good, the swell kept growing and growing, until it resulted in a monstrosity known as the "beartrap," a saddle you could hardly get out of, even if you wanted to.

But these bronc saddles were never very practical for working cowboys, even though many used them. The design was just too specific for general ranch work, and when the novelty went out of the swell fork, the trend began moving the other direction.

Once again, the trend originated in the arena, but this time design ideas came from ropers, whose needs were exactly the opposite of those of the bronc riders. Ropers, who had to jump out of the saddle and tie down an animal, needed a saddle that didn't interfere with their quick mounting and dismounting. For their purposes, the smaller the swell and cantle, the better.

Many of these "postage stamp" saddles made it out into ranch country, but they proved no more satisfactory than the bronc saddles. Again, they were too specific for the working cowboy. One extreme in design had led to another. The cowboy couldn't get out of the beartrap, but he couldn't stay on the postage stamp.

What is the design of the modern saddle? It's whatever you want and whatever you need. Today's buyer has the luxury of choosing from a wide range of designs, and the style he chooses will depend how he is using his horse—and most horse owners today are *not* using their horses to make a living on a ranch, but are riding for sport and pleasure.

There are saddles for calf ropers and dally ropers, bronc riders, barrel racers, endurance riders, and cutting horse enthusiasts. And these saddles can run all the way from "plano" (plain old, plain vanilla) to fancy varieties with hand-tooling and silver inlays.

When a ranch cowboy goes into a western store today, he is likely to find a number of saddle styles, many of which were designed for hobby horsemen and sports enthusiasts. But he can still find saddle makers tucked away in small ranching communities who specialize in saddles for the working cowboy. He can choose the tree, fork, horn, seat, and cantle he wants, and get it custom made so that it fits him like his own shadow.

Then all he has to do is figure out how he can pay for it out of cowboy wages.

The Cowboy's Boot

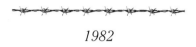

1982

THE LATE SPIKE VAN CLEVE, Montana rancher and author of several fine books, used to growl that anyone who spoke of "cowboy boots" marked himself as a dude, because in cowboy country there was only one kind of footwear.

A boot was a cowboy boot.

Texas might have more than one kind of footwear, but when a Texan speaks of wearing his boots, it's understood that he's not speaking of irrigation boots or cavalry boots, but rather the type that has come to identify the wearer as a citizen of the West.

The western or cowboy boot as we know it has been around about a hundred years, and it is said to have originated in the railheads and cowtowns of Kansas during the traildriving period. In the mid-1870s, bootmakers in Abilene, Ellsworth, Caldwell, Dodge City, and Wichita did a booming business during the summer months, turning out a type of high-heeled, high-topped boot that was favored by cowboys who had just come up the trail—most of them from Texas.

This boot, which sold for $12 to $20 a pair, was the grandfather of the modern western boot, and it replaced an earlier type that was functional but not particularly distinctive, a low-heeled model with a broad toe and stovepipe top. This earlier boot, which probably resembled today's Wellington or Dingo, was worn not only by cowboys, but by immigrants, settlers, farmers, and anyone else who wanted to keep weed seeds out of his socks.

Cowboys, who were just a little vain about their profession, latched onto the new style and adopted it as their own, and soon it became a mark of the breed.

In the cowboy's boot we find a mixture of fashion-consciousness (peacockery might be a better term) and functionalism, a tension that can be found at almost every level of cowboy life. For while the new type of boot had an air of nobility about it—stitching on the leg, high tops, and a high heel that lifted a man several inches above the dust—the design also incorporated several features that suited it for cowboy work.

The stitching on the leg was pretty, but it also made the leather more rigid, so that it didn't sag or wrinkle. The high heel elevated the wearer above the ground, but it also kept his boot from going through the stirrup when he rode a frisky horse. The pointed toe gave the boot a distinctive, streamlined appearance, but it also made it easier to slip into a stirrup.

It was the footwear of a horseman, and not necessarily fit for walking on dry land. Indeed, the more extreme designs, with two-inch underslung heels and narrow toes, were hardly fit for walking any farther than the space between the saddle shed and the bunk house. It has even been suggested that the cowboy boot was designed by a horse trader who wanted to make sure that cowboys didn't get too fond of walking.

I know a fellow who worked in Congressman Jack Hightower's office in Washington. One time a friend of his from the Panhandle called to say that he was going to spend a few days seeing the sights in the nation's capitol.

"I'd advise you to leave your boots at the hotel and wear a pair of comfortable sneakers."

The guy snorted at that. He didn't wear such things, never had and didn't intend to start now. If he couldn't see Washington in his boots, then Washington just didn't need to be seen.

The next day, after he had hiked around the various parts of the Smithsonian (which turned out to be even bigger than the court house back home), he came down with a pretty severe case of hoof problems. Derned near crippled him, in fact, and the next day he bought his first pair of sneakers. Vanity hath its limits.

One factor which used to compound the cowboy's problems in walking is that he would often buy his boots just a tad small. "Snowshoe" or "washtub" feet were never much admired in cowboy circles, and punchers had often been inclined to shrink their feet by stuffing them into snug-fitting boots.

Back in the old days, virtually every cowboy had his boots handmade by the bootmaker of his choice. He would go in once, select the type of heel, toe, leg, top, and stitching he wanted, and get his foot measured. Once the bootmaker had made a *last* (a form in the shape of the customer's foot), then the cowboy could order a new pair of boots by mail or phone, without leaving the ranch or going to the shop.

In the 1880s a pair of handmade boots might cost a $35-a-month cowhand $20, which didn't leave much of his wages for frivolity.

Today's cowboy is much more likely to buy his boots off the shelf. In a good western wear store, he will find a wide variety of styles, colors, leathers, and brand names. The type of boot he chooses will depend on what he intends to do in them.

If he does a lot of riding, he may select a boot with a tall, underslung heel, a high top to protect his legs from the chafing of the saddle, a strong heel counter that will hold a spur, and a shank that will keep its shape under work conditions.

If he is buying a boot for ground work (which might include walking fence, loading hay, and doing chores around the ranch), he will probably choose a shorter heel and a sole made of synthetic material. Leather soles get slick after a while and are hard to walk on, and leather doesn't hold up as well as man-made materials to the mud and manure of a cow lot.

The leather in a work boot is important. Some leathers are easily torn and don't hold up to heavy work, while others are known for their strength and durability. Mulehide is soft but durable. Oil-tanned cowhide is good in a work boot because it can be treated with neats foot oil instead of polish. When you're oiling up your saddle and tack, you can take a swipe across your boots and give them a coat of water proofing.

Bullhide and sharkskin are probably the toughest of all leathers, and you can hardly wear them out, even when you're looking for an excuse to buy a new pair of boots.

If you're shopping for a stylish boot, one that you can wear to church or to the rodeo, the range of choices is even wider. You can select such creamy-soft leathers as calf, antelope, and goatskin, or get into the real exotics, such as eel, ostrich, lizard, boa, and sea turtle.

If you happen to be proud of your Texas heritage, you'll be pleased to know that many of the mainline brands are made in your home state: Tony Lama, Sanders, Hondo, and Laramie in El Paso; Nocona in Nocona; Justin in Ft. Worth; and Lucchese in San Antonio.

There are other boot companies that are not located in Texas but appear to wish they were. For example, where would you suppose Laredo and Texas Brand boots are made? If you guessed Nashville and Lebanon, Tennessee, respectively, you're right.

But all modern cowboys don't buy their boots out of the store. Some continue to do business with the dwindling number of bootmakers in the state and get boots that are made to their own specifications. A cowboy in far West Texas once explained to me why he special-ordered his boots (at $300 a pair) from a bootmaker, when he was drawing $600 a month as a cowboy:

> I can get four or five times as much wear out of hand-made boots, so instead of buying four or five pairs of store-bought boots at a hundred bucks a throw, I invest in one pair of handmades at three hundred. In the long run it's cheaper, plus I'm getting exactly the kind of boot I want.

When the western boot first appeared a hundred years ago, it was more than just another kind of footwear. Those who wore the high-heeled, sharp-toed boots had earned the right to wear them, by roping wild cattle, sleeping outside in the rain, and wrecking a few horses. The boot was a badge of honor, part of the uniform of an elite group of professionals. When a non-member wore the boots, he did so at the risk of being ridiculed for pretending to be something he wasn't.

When I was growing up in the Panhandle in the 1950s and 1960s, this attitude was still around. We understood, without actually being told, that cowboys were something special and that one didn't wear those boots unless one had done something to earn the right.

That attitude seems a little archaic today. The Urban Cowboy phenomenon and a general revival of interest in the West has created a huge demand for boots. All at once city folks and non-cowboys discovered that wearing boots was a lot more fun than wearing wing-tip shoes, and once they made this discovery, there was no stopping them.

Today, Texans from all walks of life are wearing boots and enjoying the heck out of it. They have learned to enjoy the slap-slap of the tops against their calves, and when they pass by a mirror or a store window, they can't help taking a peek at those dandy new boots.

Working cowboys ought to understand this kind of peacockery, because they've been practicing it for a hundred years, ever since they discovered those same boots in the cowtowns of Kansas.

Part V

Ranch and Rodeo

The Pecos Rodeo:
100 Years Old

1982

BIG BLUE THUNDERHEAD CLOUDS hang over the mountains west of town, grumbling and shooting out forks of lightning. Three old fellow gaze off at the storm. "Reckon it'll hit here?" one asks.

"Sure. It always rains on rodeo night, never fails."

The others nod, lift their hats, and wipe away trickles of sweat. It is seven o'clock in the evening, but still West Texas hot.

The three old timers are sitting in the empty grandstands. They forget the storm and go back to talking about horses and cowboys of days gone by.

In the announcer's booth, high above the freshly plowed arena, Tom Hadley of Mason switches on the public address system and blows into the microphone. "Testing, one two three, testing, one two."

The cowboys are arriving now, dressed in boots, jeans, long-sleeved Western shirts, and cowboy hats. Some carry bronc saddles while others tote nylon bags that hold the gear of a bull rider.

"They look so young, don't they?" a woman whispers to her husband as they enter the stands.

The husband studies the cowboys. "They are young, hon. If they were any older, they'd have better sense."

The stream of human traffic through the main gate is picking up now, as spectators make their way to the seating areas on both sides of the arena. They have come from Midland and Odessa, Monahans, Kermit, Barstow, Toyah, and Balmorhea. And, of course, from Pecos, home of the Pecos Rodeo.

Some speak Spanish, others the slow, easygoing variety of Texas English that accords with empty spaces, locust-humming mesquite trees, July heat, and barbecue.

East of the arena, in the shadow of the announcer's booth, a young man in cowboy clothes leans against the pipe corral and peers at the animals inside the holding pen: two dozen monsters with horns, humps, swinging dewlaps, and loose hides.

Another cowboy walks up. "What did you draw?"

"Frankenstein."

They study Frankenstein, a living, breathing nightmare wrapped in a tiger-striped skin, with two-foot horns, long ears, a hump over his shoulder, and black eyes filled with animal cunning and animal vengeance.

When God started building bulls, He never intended for them to be ridden. But young men will try it, for reasons their mothers will never understand.

That is how rodeo got started, young men doing things their mothers couldn't understand. And there is good reason for thinking that the first rodeo ever held in the United States occurred right here in Pecos, Texas, in 1883.

Pecos was a raw, wild West Texas cowtown back then, with more saloons than churches. Tradition holds that one day in June, cowboys from the Lazy Y and Hashknife outfits gathered in front of Red Newell's Saloon and got into an argument about which ranch had the best ropers and riders.

Someone suggested that a contest be held on the Fourth of July to settle the matter once and for all. The public would be invited to watch and prizes would be given to the winners. It seemed a good idea, and the word was passed around.

On July 4 a crowd of 1,000 spectators showed up to watch cowhands from the Hashknife, W, Lazy Y, and NA ranches compete for $40 in prize money.

There were no bucking chutes, no holding pens, or grandstands for the event. The contest was held on a flat near the courthouse, and spectators on horseback formed a circle that opened toward the prairie.

At that contest in Pecos, no one had ever heard the word "rodeo," since it wouldn't make its appearance into the English language until some forty years later. Nor had anyone ever heard of the modern rodeo events such as bull riding, barrel racing, or bareback bronc riding.

The events at this first-ever rodeo were saddle-bronc riding and steer roping, and they were not so much "events" as they were daily chores of ranch cowboys of the time. Ranch work of the day required that a man be able to ride an unfriendly, unwilling, cantankerous horse, and once he had the bronc "rode" and schooled, he had to be able to go out on the unfenced expanse of West Texas and impose his will upon horned bovine critters who didn't want to be imposed upon.

He did this with his rope: pitching his loop around the horns, flipping his slack around the animal's back legs, turning the horse away at a sharp angle, tripping the critter off his feet, and then tying him down with a short piece of rope.

These were the two events at the first Pecos rodeo, and they have remained an integral part of rodeo ever since.

But rodeo, like the town of Pecos where it was born, has changed and adapted to different times. Rodeo is no longer a roping and riding contest among ranch cowboys, but rather a national sport that draws professional athletes and offers the best of them an opportunity to make a living at it.

And for a few—the Tom Fergusons, Leo Camarillos, Don Gays, and Roy Coopers—there is even the chance for fame and fortune.

Today's rodeo competitor might have grown up on a ranch in Texas, New Mexico, or South Dakota. Or, like Charlie Sampson who won the bull riding at Pecos in 1982, he might have grown up in the Watts section of Los Angeles, or in the Bronx, New York, as did another bull rider named Bobby DelVecchio.

The modern rodeo competitor has his own professional organization (the Professional Rodeo Cowboys Association, Inc., or PRCA, with offices in Colorado Springs), his own trade newspaper (ProRodeo Sports News), and his own Hall of Champions at PRCA headquarters.

Entries for the hundreds of PRCA-sanctioned rodeos held in the United States every year are now handled by computer at PRCA headquarters in Colorado Springs. There, the Professional Rodeo Communications of America (PROCOM) matches competitors, stock, and positions through a central entry office, eliminating the error and chaos of previous years when a cowboy had to feed quarters into a pay phone to call the rodeo committee in the next town and find out what he had drawn and when he was up.

Today, if a young cowboy wants to learn rodeo but hasn't grown up on a ranch, he can study his trade at rodeo schools taught by seasoned veterans. The first roping school was started in 1954 by Toots Mansfield of Big Spring, the seven-time world champion calf roper who began winning money at the Pecos rodeo in the early 1940s.

In 1963, Jim Shoulders, one of the great bronc and bull riders of all time, opened the first riding school at Henryetta, Oklahoma. Shoulders, like Mansfield, won his share of prize money at Pecos.

It is eight o'clock now. The stands are almost full and people are still streaming through the gates. Producers Mack Altizer and Bernis Johnson have loaded the bucking chutes with bulls for the first riding event and are attending to last minute details.

Quail Dobbs, the 1978 PRCA clown of the year, is dressed for his night's work (face paint and baggy pants and a black derby hat), and is sitting on the steps of his trailer, autographing programs for some of his fans. In a few minutes, he will be sassing the bulls in the arena and relieving tension with his antics.

Somewhere in the crowd, the young cowboy who drew Frankenstein is loosening up, talking to himself, going over the bull's patterns and habits. When the chute gate opens, he will try to stay on the bull for eight seconds, holding on with one hand to a rope around its middle. He will be disqualified if he is bucked off or if his free hand touches the bull. If he makes it to the whistle, he will be scored by judges who give points on the difficulty of the ride and how well he maintains his balance.

The bull riding is one of seven PRCA rodeo events. Saddle bronc riding might be called rodeo's classic contest, since it grew out of the cowboy's work in the old West. Mounted in a PRCA-approved saddle which has stirrups but no horn, the cowboy holds a six-foot braided rein in one hand and keeps the other hand free. When the chute gate opens, he tries to get in time with the bronc and spur him from the shoulders back to the saddle. The rider is scored on the smoothness of his ride and on how well he has spurred the horse.

Bareback bronc riding is the youngest of the riding events, and here the cowboy has no saddle. Instead, he is attached to his mount by a ten-inch-wide leather surcingle with a suitcase-like handle, into which he jams his gloved hand. As in the saddle bronc event, riders in the bareback riding are scored on their balance and spurring action. But where the saddle bronc rider maintains an upright position, the bareback rider often appears to be lying down on the horse's back, spurring up and down near the horse's neck.

Like the saddle bronc riding, the roping events (calf, steer, and team roping) trace back to the work of the old-time cowboy, and each of these timed events requires teamwork between contestant and horse.

In calf roping, the contestant must rope a three-to-four hundred pound calf, flank him to the ground, and tie three feet with a pigging string. When the ropers hands go into the air, the clock is stopped.

Steer roping presents the contestant with a different technical problem: catching and tripping down a grown steer on the run. Then, while the horse holds the rope tight and keeps the animal prone, the cowboy dismounts and ties the steer down.

Team roping offers the same technical problem—controlling a grown steer—but with two ropers instead of one. The first catches the steer by the horns and turns off to one side, while the second rides in and catches both hind legs in his loop. When the horses turn and face each other, and the steer goes to the ground, the clock stops.

Steer wrestling or bulldogging was never part of everyday ranch work, but was more of an exhibition sport that started in the arena. In this event, the contestant and a "hazer" keep a big steer running in a straight line. The contestant slips off his horse at full speed, grabs the steer by the horns, and pulls the head around until the animal falls to the ground.

Although women's barrel racing is not one of the seven PRCA contests (the ladies have their own organization, the Women's Professional Rodeo Association), most modern rodeos feature this timed event. Running a cloverleaf pattern around the three barrels requires expert riding and a fast, well-trained horse. A wide turn around a barrel adds precious time to a run, but if a barrel is knocked over it adds a five-second penalty—which is impossible to make up.

Back at the Pecos rodeo arena, Tom Hadley's voice comes over the public address system. "All right, ladies and gentlemen, we're just about ready for the grand entry and another evening of America's favorite sport. Welcome to Pecos, Texas, where it all began 100 years ago."

Then conversation stops, and spectators, bull riders, ropers, flag carriers, pickup men, reporters, and clowns remove their hats, pause, and listen to the singing of the national anthem. Off to the west, thunder growls over the mountains as Old Glory flaps in a soft West Texas breeze.

The old men in the stands were wrong. Maybe it "always" rains on rodeo night, but this time it didn't. It wouldn't dare, not on the world's oldest rodeo.

Texas Ranch
Roundup

— ※— ※— ※— ※— ※— ※— ※— ※—

1982

(In August of 1982 I attended the Texas Ranch Roundup in Wichita Falls, Texas, and wrote the following story for Texas Highways magazine. At that time, it was the only ranch rodeo I knew about, and the first I had ever attended. Since that time the idea has spread to other states and other parts of Texas).

MANY PEOPLE THINK OF ranching and rodeo as very similar, maybe even identical. After all, rodeo began as a display of working cowboy skills, and ranching and rodeo both involve horses, cattle, cowboys, and ropes.

But while rodeo and ranching grew out of the same common root, over the years they have gone in different directions. Rodeo has developed into a highly competitive, polished, and professionalized discipline that molds both men and horses into specialized athletes.

Ranching, on the other hand, has made a few compromises to changing times and technologies, but the basic functions of the rancher are the same today as they were a hundred years ago: to convert grass into beef and to make a living selling cattle. All the skills of the ranch cowboy are directed toward these goals.

In other words, ranch ain't rodeo and rodeo ain't ranch. They are so different, in fact, that over the years friction has built up between the two, a kind of family feud that has grown out of the differences in temperament.

We might say that the typical rancher is conservative by nature. He is accustomed to long periods of silence and has a natural aversion to noise. His pace appears to be slow and deliberate because it derives from the rhythms of livestock and the seasons of the year.

The rancher is work-oriented. Work is his medium of expression, his art form, his highest source of pleasure. His approach to cattle work was shaped by older men who drilled economy of movement into his head: "Don't trot your horse if you can walk him. Don't chouse the cattle. Don't make noise in the herd. Don't run pounds off the stock."

To this man, the thunder and lightning of a modern rodeo is alien. Its basic function is not to sharpen the skills of working cowboys, but to entertain a crowd with exhibitions of athletic ability. Our rancher might enjoy watching a rodeo from the stands, but he certainly doesn't want his cowboys playing rodeo on his ranch with his cattle and horses, and if he runs a help-wanted ad in a livestock paper, he is likely to say, "Rodeo cowboys need not apply."

Cattle ranchers got soured on rodeo back in the Twenties and Thirties, at a time when the concept of rodeo was changing. Before, a rodeo had been a local affair, with cowboys from neighboring ranches coming together on a holiday or a Saturday afternoon to compete in ranch-related events.

But as rodeo became more popular, ranch cowboys learned they could make more money roping calves or riding broncs in the arena than they could nursemaiding cows on the range. To sharpen their skills, they began roping the boss's cattle and bucking out the ranch horses.

This infuriated the ranchers, who perceived, correctly, that the goals of the rodeo-minded cowboys differed from the goals of a pounds-and-profit cattle operation. The split this difference created between rodeo and ranching exists to this day, and has grown wider as rodeo has become more professionalized.

Some old-timers can still remember the rodeos of yesterday, when whole families came and camped for several days, ate dinner on the ground, told stories around the campfire at night, and watched their dads and brothers and cousins ride and rope against cowboys from other outfits. The old-timers who can still call up those warm memories are likely to mourn the passing of the amateur, ranch-against-ranch kind of rodeo.

But they needn't mourn. It's coming back.

Several years ago Mike McAfee, a Budweiser distributor in Wichita Falls, got an idea. Why not go back to the old style of rodeo and get some of the famous old-line Texas ranches to send their cowboys to compete in ranch-related events?

He put together a proposal and sent it to the directors of the nearby Waggoner Ranch, the 510,000 colossus headquartered at Vernon. The directors liked it, so McAfee sent out brochures to thirty big ranches in Texas.

The initial response was not overwhelming or particularly enthusiastic, even though McAfee proposed to give all the proceeds to charity. The ranch owners were wary. The old schism between ranch and rodeo ran wide and deep, and McAfee had to do a lot of traveling and talking to convince the ranch people that the idea would work.

At last he got twelve ranches to commit themselves to it. A ranch committee was formed, and this committee drew up a list of events and rules. And in August 1981, Wichita Falls held its first-ever Texas Ranch Roundup.

"We had high expectations," says Mike McAfee, "but we never dreamed it would go over this big. The ranchers just love it. It's a reunion to them. And the crowd loves it. It's unique."

The 1981 Ranch Roundup was a smashing, howling, thundering success—not because it pushed Budweiser into the number one position in the local beer market (it did), not because a nice chunk of money was raised for charity (it was), not because any world records were shattered (they weren't), but because the entire weekend was suffused with a kind of innocent charm that is hard to find these days.

In 1982, thirteen ranches sent cowboys and horses to the event: R. A. Brown Ranch of Throckmorton, Coldwater Cattle Company of Amarillo, Cowan and Son Ranch of Archer City, Double U Hereford Ranch of Levelland, Lewis Ranches of Clarendon, Moorhouse Ranch Company of Benjamin, Pitchfork Land and Cattle Company of Guthrie, Renderbrook-Spade Ranch of Colorado City, Swenson Ranches of Stamford, Scharbauer Ranches of Midland, Tongue River Ranch Corporation of Spur, U Lazy S Ranch of Post, and the W. T. Waggoner Estate Ranch of Vernon.

The contestants, all working cowboys who had been with their ranches at least six months, competed in six events especially designed for this particular rodeo: saddle bronc riding, team branding, team roping, wild cow milking, team penning, and wild horse racing.

The competition was judged by a team of professional rodeo cowboys, called the Budweiser Six Pack, with points awarded to the first five teams. The ranches were also judged in several non-rodeo events which involved the ranch wives: ranch cooking, ranch queen, talent contests, and barrel racing.

At the end of the second night's performance, the points were totaled up, and a traveling trophy went to the ranch with the highest score, Lewis Ranches in 1981 and Moorhouse Ranch Company in 1982. Also, a trophy saddle was presented to the man judged the best all-around cowboy. Tom Moorhouse won in 1981, and Junior Daniels of the Pitchfork won in 1982.

The difference between the Ranch Roundup and a normal PRCA rodeo can be seen in the events. Of the six events, only team roping and saddle bronc riding are recognized on the professional circuit. The others—team branding, wild cow milking, team penning, and the wild horse race—were chosen by the ranch committee because they drew on the skills of the working cowboy.

What about steer wrestling, bareback bronc riding, and bull riding? They were omitted because they are strictly arena events that did not originate in ranch work. If a ranch cowboy needs to catch a steer in the pasture, he doesn't mount the brute from a running horse and wrestle him to the ground. That's awful hard on clothes. He uses his catch rope. If he rides a bronc, it's usually unplanned and without his consent, which means that he's in a saddle, not bareback. And ranch cowboys don't ride bulls. They get enough adventure in the course of a normal day without shopping around for more.

Team branding probably rates as the purest, most "cowboy" event at the Roundup. One team member rides into a loose herd of cows and calves, ropes a calf either by the neck or heels, and drags it out of the herd. Then two "rasslers" throw the calf to the ground and hold it while a fourth team member applies a branding iron dipped in white paint.

It is the purest event not only because this is exactly how the work is done at the spring branding, but also because it demonstrates roping techniques that originated on ranches, have been preserved on ranches, and are rarely seen outside of ranches.

This "herd roping" is distinctly different from the regular rodeo events of team roping and calf roping. Team and calf roping began in ranch work, but the technique and timing in both events have been refined by arena ropers who are competing against the clock. In these two events, speed is everything.

In herd roping, speed is less important than patience, finesse, and savvy of the cow brute. The herd roper must slip through the cattle, stirring them without stampeding them, search for an unbranded calf, and wait for a shot to materialize.

Team roping and calf roping can be learned in the arena, and masters of these events may never have set foot on a ranch. But good herd ropers are made only on ranches that still use the rope as a working tool.

The Lewis Ranches of Clarendon have won the team branding two years in a row. Their secret weapon is a modest, easygoing cowboy named Donnie Hall. Donnie is a cowboy's cowboy. He started working on the JA Ranch in Palo Duro Canyon when he was eighteen, and one can believe that his herd roping would have pleased even as harsh a critic as the founder of the JA, the ferocious, outspoken, and astute Mr. Charles Goodnight.

Watching Donnie Hall pluck calves from the herd was one of the high points of the 1982 Ranch Roundup. It was cowboy work raised to art, poetry with a rope. Donnie and his gray horse slipped through the herd as quietly as a ghost, Donnie holding a small open loop poised at his side. He didn't twirl the loop or twitch a muscle. He seemed frozen in the saddle. Nothing moved but his eyes.

He shaped the cattle until he found the shot he wanted. Then, with a flick of his wrist, he laid a perfect trap under the calf's belly, gathered up both hocks, and headed for the branding fire.

We might imagine that somewhere in the spirit world, old man Goodnight nodded his grizzled head and muttered, "That boy's a hand."

Indeed he is; also a living repository of a lore and a life that began in the brush country of South Texas after the Civil War, went up the trail to Kansas in the 1870s, and took root on the big ranches of West Texas and the Panhandle in the 1880s. It isn't likely that Donnie Hall's name will ever become a household word. Neither will the names of Tom or John Moorhouse of the Moorhouse Ranch, Sam Whitley of the U Lazy S, Bob

Moorhouse and Junior Daniels of the Pitchfork, or Bob Northcutt of the Renderbrook-Spade.

But they're something better: the best ranch cowboys in Texas, and that means the world.

Part VI

Animals

People and
Animals

〜✳〜✳〜✳〜✳〜✳〜✳〜✳〜✳〜

1983–93

IF YOU DRIVE DOWN LBJ Freeway in North Dallas and look at the glass and stone skyscrapers that have sprung up in what used to be empty fields, you begin to appreciate the enormous difference between a rancher's view of the world and that of urban dwellers.

The people who work in those buildings are shielded from most of the forces that shape a rancher's life: wind, sun, heat, cold. They are also living in a world that does not contain animals. Just one of those enormous glass structures may hold more people than an entire town in my part of the country, but not a single animal—not a horse or a dog, not a mouse, not even a fly.

Just think of the changes that have occurred in the space of one or two generations. We have gone from a life that revolved around cattle, horses, pigs, chickens, and dogs, into one where animals are totally absent in the workplace, and perhaps in the home as well.

In all of human history, there has never been another culture that has been so successful at freeing itself from the stink and the mess and the burden of caring for animals, and from the unpleasant but necessary tasks involved in turning them into a source of food. No group of people who came before us has ever had the experience of living in a world without animals—their rhythms, idiosyncracies, compulsions, insights, heroism, demands, their stupidity and their wisdom.

We are the first people in human memory to do it. We're doing it right now, and I suspect that it's changing us in ways we don't realize.

In years past, animals probably exerted more influence on human thought and behavior than anyone ever suspected. They acted as a mediator, a point of contact, between people and the earth, reminding us of our source and of our place in the system of biology. To use a common expression, they brought us down to earth.

So what happens when we no longer have a dog or cow or a chicken to bring us down to earth? We begin losing contact with the processes that govern life in the natural world, and our perceptions of animals and humans begin to change. We perceive animals as *better* than they actually are, and perceive ourselves as *worse*.

Notice, for example, the way animals are portrayed in books and animated cartoon programs for children. Here, the "animals" have been so highly idealized that they aren't animals at all. They might *look* like animals but they think and talk like humans, while the human characters are often portrayed as villains and wicked figures of authority—villains who set mouse traps for little Mickeys and Minnies, villains who force horses to work and cows to give milk and chickens to lay eggs, villains who threaten to butcher cattle and hogs, and who never seem to understand the goodness and innocence of the "animal" characters.

Since all the "good" characters have no foundation in biology, they are never troubled by the problem of what to eat, and from this lofty position, they are able to pass judgment on the human "bad guys" who use animals for work and as a source of food.

At first glance, there doesn't seem to be anything particularly wrong with allowing children to identify with animal characters—except that the animals *aren't* animals. They are fantasies that have come from the human imagination. Not only do they lack the unpleasant qualities that biology imposes upon all creatures, but they have been given a level of sweetness and perfection that is simply unattainable in this world, against which human beings will inevitably come out looking cruel and insensitive.

In watching animated movies and a few cartoons, including the CBS version of my book, *Hank the Cowdog*, I have begun to suspect that the people who make cartoons not only have a shallow understanding of animals, but also that they *dislike people*. How else can you explain the current of misanthropy that runs through the cartoons?

When humans are consistently portrayed as spoilers, ravagers, killers, eaters, figures of discipline and authority, and villains of other stripes; and when the so-called "animals" come across as innocent victims, what conclusion can you draw? *Animals are good and people aren't.*

Animals are good because they don't spoil the earth with industrial waste and forest fires; because they don't work as school principals or policemen or other figures of authority; because, unlike human parents, they are nice all the time and don't force discipline upon children; and because they don't kill other animals and eat their flesh—in cartoons, of course.

Cartoon "animals" have become modern man's image in a mirror: exactly what we are, only backwards. In other words, exactly what we *aren't* and can never be. Cartoon "animals" express our disappointment in who we are. In reverse, they capture our failures and our stupidities and our confusion about our place in the natural order of things. This cartoon view of reality, which our little ones are absorbing every Saturday morning, raises a question of which adults might not even be aware:

If humans are so bad and animals are so good, then wouldn't the world be better if the humans just . . . went away?

This is the kind of question that springs from a young mind which follows adult logic to conclusions that adults probably never intended, and would surely disavow if it occurred on a conscious level. But it doesn't. It is a hidden message, and a disturbing message. A child can overcome the bad effects of poverty, racial discrimination, a learning disability, or a physical handicap. These temporary roadblocks can be conquered by an exertion of will. But human self-hatred? It goes right to the heart of what every child is, will always be, and cannot help being: *a member of the human race.*

There is no proper response except apathy and despair.

Where does this human self-hatred come from? It comes from glass and stone buildings in large American cities, where the people who write children's stories brood over urban sprawl, rising crime, world hunger, traffic congestion, and the other symptoms of our flawed stewardship over this planet. Faced with the mess we have made, the writers transfer their weariness onto cartoon characters, giving the "animals" all the attributes of wisdom, innocence, and goodness that humans so obviously lack.

What is missing here is any sense of biological reality, any basis for an honest comparison. The fact is that people are not as bad, nor are animals as good, as they are portrayed, but writers who live apart from animals don't know it. In their antiseptic, animal-free world, they see only human folly and human failure.

I have spent a good part of my adult life living and working with livestock, and I have come to realize that there is a kind of wisdom that comes from our association with animals. They teach us patience. They force a sense of humor upon us. We learn that all creatures are only as good as what they eat and drink, and that this applies to humans no less than to livestock. But perhaps the most valuable lesson that animals can teach us is that they are flawed, just as we are. We are all part of the same creation. Our feet are planted in the same dust, we are driven by the same appetites, and biology has marked us all for better and for worse.

We find a good illustration of this in the relationship between mankind and horses. Like marriage, it is an often bumpy affair between two imperfect creatures. We humans have our flaws, which we needn't elaborate because they are so obvious, but horses have their flaws too, and anyone who has worked around them on a daily basis knows that there is nothing particularly noble about horses who are left to their own devices.

In their natural state, horses are *not* pure and innocent. Their lovemaking rituals are brief, brutal, and devoid of romance. They will beat up the weak, the crippled, and the aged, and at a feed trough, they care nothing about "animal rights."

In short, horses are petty, malicious, selfish, cruel, bullying, greedy, and lazy. Perhaps this explains the ancient bond that has brought horses and mankind together. We have many deplorable traits in common. Yet somehow, when we come together to accomplish a goal, we both make ourselves a little better and more noble.

The fact is that horses need people and people need horses, just as men need women and women need men. To discover the best in ourselves and to reach our potential on this earth, we need more than one selfish ego that has "liberated" itself from other creatures. Horses would *not* be better if they were "liberated" from people. They would be much worse. A horse dignifies himself through work. He was made to work, designed to work, yet apart from man, he lacks the will and the discipline to do anything but perform the same biological functions that motivate a tapeworm.

In the cartoon world, the discipline that mankind imposes on a horse to make him work is often depicted as cruelty. But discipline is not cruelty. Weakness, a lack of will to discipline, is the darkest cruelty of all. Masked behind simple-minded pieties, it deprives the individual, whether horse or human, of his opportunity to fulfill himself and to make a contribution to his world.

Perhaps cartoon-horses don't need discipline, but real horses do, every bit as much as people need it. People who live undisciplined lives eat too much, drink too much, watch television instead of thinking, dabble with drugs, and sink into despair. Undisciplined horses grow fat and worthless, and often develop neurotic symptoms such as chewing on wooden fences.

Alas, real animals are prone to many of the same flaws that afflict the human race, and if we want to find perfection and innocence, we should hope for a better deal in the next life—not seek perfection in cartoon fantasies.

This same confusion about mankind's relationship with animals was an underlying theme in two successful movies, *City Slickers* and *Babe*.

In *City Slickers*, several executives from Los Angeles go to a dude ranch to relax. Upon their arrival, Billy Crystal and his pals are neophytes, city dudes. They must be taught to ride and rope. Within days, they transform themselves from bumbling amateurs into competent cowboys—a process which, in the actual West, requires years of practice and experience. But this is Hollywood, and by the end of the movie, they have become better cowboys than the cowboys who taught them.

The city slickers not only surpass their teachers in the skills of cowboying, but they also prove themselves to be *morally superior*. As the movie progresses, the actual cowboys are portrayed as brutal, insensitive, uncaring, and cruel to animals, while the dudes establish themselves as paragons of virtue. The final triumph of Billy Crystal's moral superiority comes when he returns home to Los Angeles—*with an orphan calf in his car*!

This gesture suggests that Crystal has changed the relationship between man and beast, simply because *he cares about cattle*. He refuses to accept that cattle are mere livestock, animals that serve mankind by providing meat, milk, and labor. The calf has become Crystal's *friend*.

Fifty years ago, when most American movie-goers had some experience dealing with livestock animals, this movie, and particularly its sappy ending, would have been laughed out of the theaters. Viewers should have known that: 1. human beings have been using cattle as a source of hides, meat, milk, tallow, and labor for something like ten thousand years; 2. this relationship has allowed both species to survive and prosper; and 3. Billy Crystal is alive today because his ancestors had sense enough to *eat* their cattle instead of trying to form relationships with them.

The audience would have known that baby calves grow into adults who weigh a thousand pounds, are stupid, messy, and destructive; don't make good pets, don't want people-friends, and don't fit into the lifestyle of suburban Los Angeles.

And they would have wondered about the mental condition of an adult male who didn't know all this.

But that was back in the days when Americans lived with animals. Today, we don't. We have lost all memory of hunger, hardship, animal husbandry, and food preparation. Fat and well fed, we have fallen into sentimentality and childish longings. *City Slickers* appealed to our longing to live in a world apart from the rhythms and relationships of biology.

Another movie which explored the same theme was *Babe*. Most critics and movie-goers found it charming, innocent, and refreshing, but this was another movie that couldn't have been shown fifty or sixty years ago—say, during the Depression of the thirties. In those dark times, many Americans kept hogs and there was never any doubt why. *They ate them.*

Viewers who were battling starvation in 1933 and using their hogs as a means of feeding their families would have noticed something in *Babe* that was lost on the well-fed Americans who saw it in 1995. It was not just a movie about a talking pig. It was a movie about a talking pig who didn't want to be made into bacon—in other words, a pig seeking to change the traditional relationship between humans and hogs.

Babe wanted to opt out of the food chain.

When the movie was shown to American audiences in 1995, this was an almost subliminal message. It occurred through the device of making a pig the hero of the story, and once again, showing humans as evil, greedy, and cruel. Had the movie been shown in 1933, the message would not have been hidden at all. It would have been perfectly obvious, and would have been seen as perfectly ridiculous.

During the Depression, people weren't looking for friends in their hogpens. Their relationship with their pigs was simple and unclouded by moral ambiguity: "I feed you, I care for you, and then you feed my children."

Once again, the sentimentality of these movies comes from glass and stone buildings in large American cities, where people write screenplays about "animals" that are better than people—in clean offices where the sudden appearance of a real Babe or Billy Crystal's bovine buddy would bring the police.

We live in a golden age, a period of unprecedented peace and prosperity. We are detached from the raising, gathering, and processing of our food, which means that we are detached from nature. We can expound on the background radiation of the Big Bang, the arrangement of genes, and the movement of theoretical particles at the quantum level, yet . . . nobody knows how to kill and pluck a chicken anymore, and many of our citizens have come to think of it as morally wrong.

This may fall into the category of Good Problems To Have, but if the record of human experience on this planet has anything to teach us, it is that things change. The combination of nature and human nature has a way of shuffling the deck and redealing the cards.

Our prosperity will not last forever. The day will come when our children wake up hungry, and when that occurs, we will be forced to remember and relearn the ancient relationship between people and animals.

People who wish to survive and keep their culture alive should not lose contact with animals.

The Mysterious
Lesser Prairie Chicken

1979

ON A QUIET SPRING morning in some parts of Beaver County, Oklahoma, you can step outside around sunrise and hear a strange sound in the distance, one that can be heard in very few places in the United States.

The sound is hard to describe and almost impossible to reproduce in written language. Actually, there are two different sounds. One is a kind of gobble or "blup-blup," and the other a loud, staccato cackle.

When cowboys along the Beaver River hear that sound, they know that spring has arrived and that the lesser prairie chicken has gone to its booming ground.

Biologists tell us that prairie chickens, members of the grouse family, belong to the genus *Tympanuchus* and are divided into two species: the lesser (*pallidicinctus*) and the greater (*cupido*).

The differences between the greater and the lesser prairie chicken are more a matter of habitat and biology than appearance. The lesser is slightly smaller than the greater and shows more brown in its plumage. While the greater is found as far north and east as Minnesota and Illinois, the lesser is confined to arid and semi-arid climates of the Southwest.

The greater prairie chicken is the most abundant and widespread member of the prairie chicken clan, which includes not only the lesser, but also Attwater's prairie chicken of the Texas Gulf Coast and the heath hen of coastal New England, which has been extinct since 1933.

The lesser prairie chicken has suffered from our expanding civilization. As early as 1909, Theodore Roosevelt recommended a closed hunting season on the bird, but even with a closed season it continued to decline in population.

Unlike the passenger pigeon, which was hunted into extinction, the prairie chicken was diminished by human influx, farmland development, and a disturbance of his natural habitat. Numbers declined rapidly during World War I when large areas of grassland were broken out and put into crop production, and the drouths of the 1930s and 1950s, combined with overgrazing, cut even deeper into the population.

Today, the lesser prairie chicken can be found in large numbers in certain areas of Texas, Oklahoma, Colorado, New Mexico, and Kansas— places that still have large areas of prairie country. There, the bird is secure enough to be hunted as a game bird. But these areas are his last stronghold, and if the day should come when they fall under the plow, the lesser prairie chicken will probably disappear.

From 1974 to 1978 I managed a ranch in Beaver County, Oklahoma, one of five counties in the western part of the state that contained stable populations of the lesser prairie chicken. On this ranch, the old prairie chicken was one of the characters we saw every day. He belonged to the sandhill and sagebrush country, along with the coyote, jackrabbit, kangaroo mouse, and rattlesnake, and it wouldn't have been the same without him.

The bird thrived in that country north of the Beaver River because the range had never been disturbed and thus continued to provide him with the native vegetation he required for survival.

I doubt that the lesser prairie chicken could ever be hunted into extinction on his native range. He is simply too wary, suspicious, and elusive. I have walked for miles and hours through sage and skunkbrush, have seen scores of birds, and have never fired a shot.

Unless he flies, you will never see him, so perfectly does he blend into his surroundings. And when he does fly, it is usually at a distance of forty yards, almost as if he has calculated the range of a shotgun. A dog working out front will simply flush him sooner.

Hunters who don't mind walking their legs off and going home with an empty game bag might stalk the prairie chicken on his native ground, but those who prefer taking home some birds have learned to hunt them in grain fields adjacent to the pasture land.

In this respect, the lesser prairie chicken has been very successful in adapting to the human population. His weakness as a species lies in the delicate and complex balance of his habitat. In a study of the lesser prairie chicken, conducted in Beaver County, Dr. Robert Earl Jones pointed out that the lesser prairie chicken requires a combination of short vegetation on tight clay soils, and half-shrub vegetation on sandy soils.

The bird chooses a different habitat for each of several life activities, such as feeding, day roosting, night roosting, breeding, and nesting. While he may rest and feed in the cover of skunkbrush on the sandhills, he conducts his courtship, or "booming," on open ground covered with buffalo and gramma grasses.

Furthermore, his habitat will vary with the season of the year, as his source of food changes from insects in the spring and summer, to seeds in the fall and winter. If this balance is disturbed, if one of these habitats disappears, then the lesser prairie chicken cannot survive.

Fortunately, favorable conditions existed in our country, and the lesser prairie chicken seemed to be doing well. I was glad, because I found him a fascinating, puzzling, mysterious bird. You can't live around the lesser prairie chicken without being drawn into a study of him. I wasn't a bird watcher by habit, but I watched the prairie chicken.

He was a hard bird to figure out. I rode many a mile on horseback across pasture land that I knew was heavily populated with prairie chickens. I saw countless nests of doves and field larks, yet I never saw a prairie chicken nest, and only once did I ride upon a chick.

The chick was mobile enough to run, and even though I dived off my horse and searched a wide area, I didn't find a nest where he might have been living.

Dr. Jones, who spent two years studying both greater and lesser prairie chickens in Oklahoma, suffered the same frustration. "A total of 272 acres of possible lesser prairie chicken nesting cover was checked," he wrote. "Not one nest was found in this area." Later, he discovered one nest. He stumbled onto it by accident and found it abandoned.

That the prairie chicken could be so clever at concealing her nest is not only frustrating, but also a source of embarrassment to scientists and cowboys who take pride in their powers of observation.

And then there is the contradictory nature of the bird. The lesser prairie chicken lives a life of paradox. On the one hand, he is so shy that he can hardly be observed at rest. Yet in the spring of the year, he becomes conspicuous, noisy, flamboyant, vulnerable, obvious, and exposed. This occurs during the breeding season, when the birds gather on their booming grounds and perform the rites for which they are best known.

On the 5000 acre ranch I managed, I discovered five booming grounds. They all sat on high ground and were covered with short-grass vegetation which would not conceal a cowchip, much less a bird the size of a pheasant. On this exposed ground, the prairie chickens danced, hopped, cackled, chased, and gobbled, and seemed oblivious to the rest of the world.

I often drove a pickup to within twenty yards of the booming grounds, and while my presence seemed to disturb them for a few minutes, they soon returned to their business, as though I wasn't there.

Then, in mid-June, they left their booming grounds and went to their nests, and I might not see one for a month. Like drunks after a long night of debauchery, they retired to quieter things.

If the cowboy has a hard time figuring out these birds, he shouldn't feel too bad about it. Dr. Kenneth Stromborg, assistant professor of range and wildlife management at Texas Tech, tried to study the lesser prairie chicken in the country south of Lubbock.

Because the birds were so secretive, he trapped a number of them and equipped them with tiny solar-powered radio transmitters which sent out signals to a portable scanner. Even with this space-age technology, "The research studies which began about eighteen months ago have yielded as much conflicting data as they have enlarged the knowledge of the prairie chicken."

So mark one up for the old prairie chicken. He doesn't want us snooping around in his business, and so far he's come out the winner.

Dogs and Coyotes:
An Ancient Bond

1998

IT IS SIX O'CLOCK IN the morning and dark. Outside my office in the bunkhouse, I can hear our three dogs barking at something in the pasture. I listen closer and notice that one of the voices has a high-pitched, staccato ring to it.

For a moment I am puzzled. Which of our dogs barks that way? Then I realize it's not the bark of a dog. It's a coyote. Our dogs are carrying on a conversation with one of their distant cousins.

This conversation occurs quite often on our Panhandle ranch and I always find it fascinating to speculate on what sort of information is being exchanged.

Begin with the fact that, at first glance, coyotes and dogs appear to be very similar. Someone from another world might even see them as the same animal. Coyotes have sharper noses, sharper ears, and bushier tails than your average dog, but in an animal kingdom that contains spiders, elephants, whales, and worms, those are pretty small differences.

The interesting thing is that, for all their outward similarities, dogs and coyotes are keenly aware of their differences. A few years back, I conducted a little experiment. A neighboring rancher had given me a coyote pup, a little fur ball that I could hold in the palms of my hands. I called my dogs over and introduced them to the new kid, thinking they might all get along and I could raise the pup alongside my dogs.

Well, that didn't last long. The dogs sniffed the pup. The pup sniffed the dogs. The pup uttered a growl which raised the hair on the backs of the dogs. A moment later, they vanished. I tried to call them back, but they wanted no more of that coyote pup. Though he was only a few weeks old, the pup seemed to share those sentiments.

There was no fooling them and my efforts to cobble up a little friendship ended in failure. Their first impression was not of their similarities, but of their differences.

And yet there is a bond between coyotes and dogs, something that keeps tugging at their minds. If they were completely different, they would ignore one another. Our dogs don't pay much attention to wild turkeys, roadrunners, turtles, crows, or buzzards that venture close to the house. But they're *always* aware when coyotes are near.

And their response is never casual. The presence of a coyote puts them on Full Alert. They become nervous and excited. Sometimes they pace around the porch, grumbling and growling. Sometimes they hide behind the porch furniture, where they whine and tap their tails. Sometimes they go charging away from the house, making brave noises, but somehow they never make it past the gravel driveway.

Oftentimes, they will bark back and forth in the night, as they are doing at this moment. The novelist in me can't resist searching for words, thoughts, and motives. Maybe the coyotes are expressing some regret that they will never know the comforts of a home—a job, a nice porch to defend, free food, kind words, pats on the head, human companionship.

And the dogs? Perhaps they feel a sense of loss for something their ancestors gave up ten thousand years ago, when they left the wild and linked their destinies with those of human beings. The yipping of a coyote stirs memories of perfect freedom and the luxury of a life unencumbered by manners and duties.

I think there is something to this speculation, and somehow it makes me feel closer to both dogs and coyotes. What could be more human, after all, than to spend all night moaning about the things you aren't, can't do, and don't have?

Part VII

This and That

Black Mesa

1983

WE ROSE AT 4:30 in the morning and fed the horses. There was a fall crispness in the air and a patch or two of frost on the weeds, reminding us that winter was not far away.

The moon was high, its silver light making phantoms and gargoyles on the rocky face of Black Mesa, a silent, looming presence one half mile north of the adobe ranch house.

Around five, we saw headlights approaching from the east, winding up the valley of the Dry Cimarron River, and one-by-one the cowboy crew pulled up in front of the house, parked their pickup-trailer rigs, and went into the house for coffee.

They left their chaps and hats at the door and bid good morning to Tanya, who pointed her wooden spoon toward the coffee pot and turned her attention back to the four frying pans on the stove.

These were the neighbors—Ben, Steve, Jay, Fred, Jack, and Monte Joe. They came this morning, some driving as far as twenty dirt-road miles, to help Floyd gather 350 steers off the mesa and bring them down into the valley.

Black Mesa is not the name of a town or a post office or a telephone exchange. It is a natural formation, a rocky plateau that vaults some 500 feet above the headwaters of the Cimarron River, between Folsom, New Mexico, and Kenton, Oklahoma.

It is also a community of sturdy ranch people who may live in Oklahoma, New Mexico, or Colorado, but whose lives are joined by the splendid isolation of this big, rough country.

Floyd and Tanya, who lived just across the state line in New Mexico, got their mail out of Folsom; their phone service out of Kenton; sent their daughter to school in Clayton, sixty miles to the south; bought their groceries in Dalhart, Texas; and listened to the weather report on a radio station out of Lamar, Colorado.

For a while we sat around the table, talking of weather, markets, grass conditions, horses, people in the "neighborhood," those whose lives were shaped by the mesa, until Tanya called us to come into the kitchen and fill our plates.

"I hope I fixed enough," she said, as we stared in amazement at platters piled high with scrambled eggs, bacon, ham, sausage, biscuits, gravy, and hash brown potatoes.

We ate the good food and washed it down with hot coffee, knowing that lunch might be eight or ten hours away.

After breakfast, Floyd and I went out and saddled our horses. We could hear the other men moving about, their spurs jingling in the dark as they unloaded their horses and talked to them in a typical cowboy manner.

"Now Socks, be nice to me this morning. I know it's cold and you've got a hump in your back, but I just don't feel like peeling myself off that old hard ground."

I was a visitor on the crew and would be riding a tall bay horse I had never ridden before. I asked Floyd his name. "Runaway," he said, leading his dun horse over to the place where the others had gathered. He glanced around and counted cowboys. "Are we ready? Let's go."

We stepped into our cold saddles, turned up our collars, and rode east along the base of the mesa. Daylight was starting to show on the horizon when we began the long climb out of the valley, riding by ones and twos up a narrow, rocky trail that had been blasted and bulldozed out of the side of the mesa.

This trail was the only link between the two parts of the 27,000 acre ranch, the lower pastures in the valley and the high pastures on top of the mesa. A sudden winter storm could make the trail impassable and leave cattle stranded up on top for weeks.

Several times, as our horses stumbled on the rocky footing, I glanced to my left and saw nothing but thin air between the ledge and the rocks a hundred feet below. And I was riding a horse named *Runaway*?

But he turned out to be better than his name. Whatever foolish thoughts he may have had before daylight were sweated out of him by the time we reached the top.

The sun was well up on the horizon when we rode out on top, and in the clear morning air, we enjoyed a spectacular view—to the south, the twin humps of Rabbit Ears Mountain; to the west, Capulin Mountain and Sierra Grande, ancient volcanoes that stir a bit more interest in these days after the eruption of Mt. St. Helens; to the north, a yawning canyon and the foothills of the Colorado Rockies; and to the east, the valley of the Cimarron, winding its way toward a union with the Arkansas River and, ultimately, with the Father of Waters, the Mississippi.

It took us two hours to reach the point where the roundup would begin, and there we split up into twos and threes, with each group assigned a certain territory to ride. We rode off in different directions and soon split again into single riders, as each of us searched for steers among the juniper and piñon trees along the rim of the mesa.

Alone, just me and Runaway, I enjoyed the silence of this big, empty country which is the natural home of the coyote, mule deer, antelope, and bobcat, as well as an occasional black bear, elk, and mountain lion. In such a place, one's mind drifts back through history and he can almost believe that time does not exist.

As I was riding along, thinking of the people who passed through the Black Mesa country over the Cimarron Cutoff of the Santa Fe Trail, my eyes fell on something on the rocky ground. I got out of the saddle, thinking I might have stumbled upon some Indian relics. Instead, I picked up a belt of tarnished .50 caliber machine gun bullets that had never been fired, relics of the Second World War when bomber crews held gunnery practice here, shooting at barrage balloons.

Several hours later, when we had our steers gathered and strung out in a long line, I watched two Air Force fighter planes streaking at low altitude down one of the canyons. They had come from a base in Clovis, New Mexico, and they were practicing flying under enemy radar.

Perhaps that very same morning, in some remote region of the Soviet Union, a counterpart to me was watching Soviet jets perform the same maneuver, practicing ways of penetrating *our* radar.

That is an odd sensation, one minute to be herding cattle in the same manner it was done a hundred years ago, and the next to be reminded of the Reagan-Gorbachev Summit, the arms race, the awesome burden of living in the nuclear age.

Even in a place like Black Mesa, where the past is alive and palpable, the present intrudes, reminding us that we are citizens of a small planet spinning through the darkness of space.

The families who live in the shadow of Black Mesa have found ways of working together to conquer isolation and hardship. If governments could do as well, we might some day translate the aspirations of honest people into national policy.

Thoughts On
A Snowy Day

1985

TODAY IS THE FIRST day of 1985. The temperature outside is thirteen degrees and feathers of snow are falling from a lead-gray sky.

Here in my office a fire crackles in the stove. I started it with the coals of yesterday's fire, which the air-tight Jodel, a marvel of Norwegian engineering and metallurgy, kept alive through the night. To the coals I added slivers of pine and redwood, then nursed it along with small pieces of oak.

When the flames grew bold, I added large pieces of oak. Now it roars and pops and sends warm waves throughout the room.

This is a good day for thinking, looking back and looking ahead while the snowflakes pile up outside my door. Later, I will have to do something about the snow, but for now let if fall.

I have let the beagle inside to share my fire. But she is young, less than a year old, and suffers the afflictions of youth: curiosity and energy in the absence of wisdom. Instead of curling up in front of the fire and making the best of my charity, she has begun to sniff and explore the room.

Beagles are hunters. What this one is hunting for, I have no idea. We have no rabbits or skunks in this office, so I suppose she will hunt spiders and silverfish. It's in the genes, that prowling instinct, and her genes will get her into mischief.

Yes, there she goes, sniffing at a first edition of J. Frank Dobie's *A Vaquero of the Brush Country* which came from my grandfather's library. Given half a chance, she would chew it to pieces.

Scamper, go lie down in front of the fire.

Now she is shredding a paper sack. I don't care about the sack but I resent the mess. I create enough of a mess just occupying this space every morning, making my fires and pots of coffee and leaving a trail of books and papers behind whatever ideas I'm following.

Foolish dog. She has a good deal going here, but she may not be smart enough to take advantage of it. I'm sure that to her dog mind, there's not much difference between a rare book and a paper sack, and in an odd sort of way, she's right. Both are made of the same wood pulp, and either one would be fun to shred.

We must credit her with a kind of common sense logic. I am being illogical by insisting there is a difference.

When you think about it, most of what we call civilization is illogical. It began when our forebears made decisions that, to a dog, would seem arbitrary and unreasonable. Someone decided that certain utterances *meant* something while others did not. Someone decided that certain marks on clay *meant* something, while other marks on the same piece of clay didn't.

Someone decided that certain patterns of sound were musical, while other patterns of sound were just noise. Someone decided that food should be taken with a fork, that fathers should not kill or breed their offspring, and that there are only ten numbers between one and ten.

We have hatched these civilized notions on a small, insignificant planet which circles a small, insignificant star, one of billions of stars in our galaxy which is only one of billions of galaxies in a Great Something we call The Universe—a terribly abstract concept which we can hardly define or describe.

Now, given this context, given our insignificance in the cosmos, doesn't it seem a bit arrogant of us to insist that the distinctions we make in the name of "civilization" mean anything at all?

On the cosmic scale or at the molecular level, the distinctions I make between a sack and a first edition Dobie are not very important. Nature doesn't care about such trifles. With quasars and black holes out there in the great beyond, we can't expect anything but cosmic indifference to our petty concerns.

Fine, except they're not petty concerns, not to me. I think the difference between a book and paper sack is fundamental, and one of the things I appreciate about being alive in this time and place is that I live among people who share this belief.

We who live in America are enjoying a precious second in time, a rare moment of order when traffic lights work and planes take off on time; when murder is frowned upon and most children needn't fear rape from their fathers; when we have medicines to ease our suffering; when we not only have enough to eat but enough to fatten ourselves; when we have the leisure time to read great books and listen to noble music—or, if we choose, to numb ourselves watching television.

Of the thousands of generations of our tribe who have walked this earth, how many have known even a single day without hunger or toothache or rotting infections—never mind the incredible luxury of having books to read? Not many.

Two hundred years ago a European king could not have bought what a welder's wife can find today in the produce section of the corner grocery store. Fifty years ago in this tough Panhandle country, the wealthiest rancher could not have had what we take for granted, that our babies probably will not die in our arms.

We are very conscious today of our power because, compared to earlier generations, we have so much of it. We have generating plants and railroads and wonders of technology and organization such as DFW Airport. We have walked on the moon and sent our first pioneers to the edge of space. We and the Soviets have the means to commit a crime of godly magnitude, the termination of biology on earth.

The danger in having so much is that we *forget* so much. It doesn't take a thermonuclear war or a catastrophic event of nature to end civilization. It is such a fragile thing that it can be destroyed by something as simple as indifference. Neglect. Loss of memory. The lack of will to make distinctions.

The subway trains in New York, covered with spray-painted names and obscenities, mindless desecrations by people who have lost the memory of chaos and the fear it ought to arouse.

The sudden increase of sexual attacks on helpless children, and worse, our apparent acceptance of it as just another crime or just another clip from the television news.

These are not just crimes against subway cars and individual children. They are crimes against humanity that change people and communities in subtle ways, eroding pride and trust and decent impulses. Even if the offenders are caught and punished, we can never recover what was taken from us—all of us.

This thing we call civilization is a line we have drawn across the water. It's something artificial and illogical that we have imposed on ourselves and our surroundings. It's real only because we believe it's real. It exists only because we demand that it exist. Logic is on the side of water that seeks its own level and waits with cosmic patience to erase all memory of our presence here.

Well, to return from cosmic thoughts, my dog has shredded the sack and has gone back to the Dobie book. Perhaps she thinks that because I allowed her to destroy the sack I will let her do the same with the book. Such small errors in judgment are what make dogs, dogs.

A Fateful
Trip

1998

THE MAJOR DECISIONS IN our lives are often made in odd ways. In the spring of 1960 a wino convinced me that I should go to college.

I was a tall, big-footed, fairly normal sophomore in Perryton High School, but a lazy student. Grades meant little to me and I was content to get by with a Gentleman's C. I didn't give much thought to college. Maybe so, maybe not. That decision lay two years in the future.

Nor did I give much thought to what I might eventually do to make a living. I don't recall that I ever considered writing as a career. Back then, we didn't know that writers could come from little towns in Texas.

If I had been forced to declare a career choice, it probably would have been ranching. I started working on ranches in the fourth or fifth grade, and by the spring of 1960 I had a steady job as a ranch hand. For the most part it was a summer job, but I also worked after school and on weekends when my boss, Henry Hale, needed a hand.

Well, one day in May Henry called me up and said, "I'm going to take the semi down to Mineral Wells and pick up a load of cedar posts. Do you want to go along for the ride?"

You bet I wanted to go, and I even managed to talk the school principal into giving me an excused absence.

Early one morning Henry pulled up in front of the house in his red Ford F-750 truck. I climbed up into the cab and we set out on the long trip down to Mineral Wells.

If you live in Perryton, all trips to Texas destinations are *long*. Located in the top right-hand corner of the Panhandle, we are closer to the state capitols of Oklahoma, Kansas, New Mexico, and Colorado than to our own capitol city of Austin, 550 miles to the southeast.

Mineral Wells, in the cedar hills north of Ft. Worth, was a six hour drive by car, somewhat longer in a semi- truck.

The first fifty miles passed without incident. Then, on the other side of Canadian, Henry pulled off the highway and stopped the truck. "Have you ever driven a semi?" No. "Well, you're fixing to learn. I don't feel good. You drive and I'll sleep. Maybe in an hour I'll feel better."

He gave me a quick lesson on split-shifting the five-speed transmission with a two-speed axle. "Oh, and these vacuum brakes don't work so great. Down-shift when you need to stop."

With that, he slumped against the passenger-side door and went to sleep, and I began my first solo flight as a truck driver. It was a little scary at first, but it was only for an hour.

The hour came and went. Henry got worse, and I drove all the way to Mineral Wells. There, we found a doctor who examined him and announced that he had . . . *measles!*

"Sleep all you can," said the doc, "stay out of the sun, and wear sunglasses to protect your eyes. And don't try to load any of those posts."

We bought Henry a pair of cheap sunglasses, and I drove the truck over hair-raising switchback gravel roads to the post yard. Henry had been told that a crew of men would be there to load the truck for us. The "crew" turned out to be a scrawny fellow with stale wine breath, skin the color of oatmeal, and a four-day growth of reddish beard.

And me. I had no idea that working in a post yard in north-central Texas was very close to a sentence to hell, but I soon found out.

These were not small posts. They were BIG posts with eight-inch butts, and a semi-trailer could hold a bunch of them. And right away I noticed something about the cedar hills of north-central Texas: the wind didn't blow and they had something called humidity.

Henry retired to the shack which served as an office, crawled into a dark corner, and suffered his own version of hell. Until then, neither of us had known that measles in adults was no laughing matter, yet everyone who heard about it thought it was pretty funny. Grown men with measles get no sympathy.

The wino and I went to work, loading the truck in the heavy windless heat. It took us seven hours, as I recall, and during that time my companion didn't talk. He loaded posts like a weary machine, keeping the same monotonous pace through the whole seven hours.

By the end of the day, every muscle in my body screamed for rest and my eyeballs were scalded by sweat, and suddenly I understood . . . *why he had decided to become a wino.* If I'd had this to look forward to every day of my life, I might have chosen that path myself.

The next day we started back to the Panhandle. Henry was still out of commission and I drove all the way home. In downtown Shamrock, I ran through a red light because, as Henry had noted, the vacuum brakes weren't so great, and we were overloaded. Fortunately, there was a gap between a car and a pickup pulling a cotton trailer, and we slipped through.

As it turned out, this trip had a powerful effect on my future. By the time I got back home, I had made some important decisions. First, I would never EVER set foot in a post yard again, and second, just to be sure I didn't, I made up my mind to go to college.

Six years later, I graduated from the University of Texas. I've become a writer and I've never gone near a post yard since that day. I owe a lot to that wino.

Easter In
Cow Country

1990

YOU CAN ASK ANY rancher in the upper Panhandle and he'll testify that the winter of 1990–91 was a dry booger.

Our last good moisture fell back in September. It was enough to make mud and get the wheat started, but after that we got only one snow.

What we got instead was two ferocious cold spells, one in January and the other about two weeks later in February. I'll remember them for a long time because of what they taught me about fixing busted pipes.

But still no moisture. By March the feed grounds were tramped down to fine powder, and every vehicle passing through the country left a trail of white caliche dust hanging in the air.

Then the March winds got cranked up. They were winds to remember, one day out of the northwest, the next out of the southwest, and the next straight out of the west. In our country any wind with "west" in its name is no friend of the rancher, and that's what we got, day after day.

The climax of this drama came on the 26th when we had straight winds that gusted up to eighty miles an hour. It blew down fences and signs, blew shingles off of roofs, blew semi-trailers off the highway, and covered everything in the camp house with a layer of dust.

So much for the $350 I'd spent putting up storm windows—"to keep the dust out," as I recall my words. I might as well have put that $350 into a new vacuum sweeper.

The wind blew down power lines and started fires. Larry Don Smith almost lost his house when a downed power line started a fire in some CRP grass, and David Seale's new barn burned to the ground in thirty minutes, taking with it all his saddles and a bunch of his hogs.

In such weather a guy begins to wonder how anything can survive in this country. This thought occurred to me on the evening of the 27th during our church's Maundy Thursday service, a service that depicts the events leading up to the crucifixion and death of Jesus.

Anyone who has attended one of these night-time services knows that the minister snuffs out a candle with the reading of each of a series of passages from the Bible, until the sanctuary is dark. The congregation leaves in silence and with thoughts of the suffering of a man who lived 2000 years ago.

I left with those thoughts, and also with thoughts of the suffering of this poor wind-scourged country—of dying wheat and withered grass, of dried up water holes and thrashed windmills, of red-eyed cows turning their backs to the cruel lash of the wind.

Things looked bleak out in the country, and maybe this was the beginning of another drought of the thirties or fifties. Maybe the grass would never come and the wind would never stop.

Two days later, on the Saturday before Easter morning, I awoke at 6:00 A.M. and looked out the window. In the first light of morning I saw that Perryton was covered with snow, and the air was filled with big wet feathers that floated straight down.

No wind, just five inches of beautiful life-giving snow.

Growing up, I often heard the old-timers say that in the Panhandle, one should never put away his long-johns and sheep lined coat until after the Easter Storm.

Well, chalk up a bulls-eye for the old-timers. This was an Easter Storm if there ever was one. Suddenly the country was soft and wearing the color of an Easter lily. I could almost hear the thirsty soil sighing with relief and the shoots of green grass pushing their way into the scented air of spring.

I could hardly wait to get down to the ranch to feed. I had visions of mud so deep that I would get stuck in the old 4x4 army truck, but my heart began to sink as I drove south of town and saw that the snow *stopped.*

Good grief, this weather system had dropped snow on five states. Couldn't it have gone another thirty miles and covered my place? What had I done? Was it something I'd said to the water pipes back in February?

Well, that just about ruined my afternoon, but we did manage to get

.30 of moisture, enough to bring out the grass in the draws and canyons. That was better than dust and wind.

On Easter morning my family and I got up before daylight, drove over to a caprock in the east pasture, and held our own little Easter sunrise service.

The valley of the Canadian River lay before us, vast and blue and silent. With a big red sun rising in the east and a big yellow moon setting in the west, we sang Easter hymns and read the Resurrection story from the Bible.

As we sang, we noticed seven mule deer on the other side of the canyon, listening to us. Our music wasn't all that great but they were patient.

It was a beautiful morning, a morning to remember. Even though we'd missed the best of the moisture, the old country was coming back and trying to green up.

The elm trees were putting out seeds. The sage was beginning to leaf out. The wild plums were bursting with white blooms.

We'd gotten enough moisture to give them hope, and maybe we could find some hope in their optimism. It was a new year, a new season.

Green grass is coming, Easter is here, alleluia!

Odd Things I've Seen
As A Cowboy

1994

ALL OF US WHO have worked around livestock have observed things that struck us as odd and out of the ordinary. I've had my share of those experiences.

Between 1974 and 1978 I was managing the Mayo ranch in Beaver County, Oklahoma. On that ranch, we ran our bulls with the cows year-round. Most of our calves hit the ground between December and April, and we branded and worked them at the spring branding. But we always had a small bunch of maybe forty or fifty calves that came later, and I took care of them at a fall branding in November or December.

At the fall branding in 1974 we paired up a small bunch of cows and calves that I wanted to haul over to the little east pasture, some two miles east of headquarters. By that time of year, the days had gotten pretty short and we always seemed to finish our work in the dark. Bill Ellzey and his cousin Tom Ellzey had come up from Wolf Creek to help me that day, and they stayed late to help me with the sorting and loading.

By the time we got the horses unsaddled and fed and the gooseneck trailer backed up to the alley, we'd used up all our daylight, which meant that we had to load the cattle in the dark. Armed with pieces of windmill rod, we drove them into the alley and started pushing them towards the trailer.

Now, these cows had a tendency to be a little snakey and you sure had to watch them close or they'd run over you. I didn't feel entirely comfortable about fooling with them in the dark, but I didn't want to leave them in the pens overnight either.

We pushed them down the alley and we could hear the front ones as they stepped up into the trailer. Then, all at once, one of the old sisters at the rear whirled around and made a run back down the alley.

I couldn't see well enough to get out of her way or to whack her on the nose with the windmill rod, and I'm guessing that she couldn't see too well either, because she came straight at me, gathered me up between her horns, carried me all the way to the east end of the alley, and let me off.

There was no big collision, no noise, no blood. One second I had been standing in the dark near my companions, and the next I was standing alone, some seventy-five feet down the alley.

I had a little trouble believing that it had actually happened, so I yelled, "Hey, did you guys just see what happened to me? That cow just picked me up and carried me all the way down here on her horns!"

I don't remember what they said, but I would guess that it was something like, "Pass that bottle over here and let us have a drink of it!"

They didn't believe me. But it happened that way, honest. And there was no bottle involved.

On that same ranch, maybe a year and a half later, I held my spring roundup in May. The evening before roundup day, we got a big thunderstorm. I was sitting out on the porch, enjoying the rain and watching the storm, and noticed that a bolt of lightning hit the barn. I didn't have any trouble noticing this because the boom that came after the flash just about knocked me out of my chair.

After the storm moved way, I walked down to the barn to see if anything had been damaged. I found the pens standing in water, but no sign of damage from the lightning strike. I was glad for that. It wasn't much of a barn to start with, just a 20' x 40' shed covered with sheet iron, but it was all I had.

Well, the crew arrived the next morning, twelve or fourteen of the usual hands, mostly neighbors with whom I had swap-out arrangements. The Ellzey boys had come up from Texas and had brought Tom's sister Jill with them.

Everyone unloaded their horses at the pens and I outlined my strategy for the roundup. We were going to gather the middle pasture, as I recall, and to get into that pasture, we had to lead our horses through the pens.

Jill Ellzey was in front of me, leading her Cookie mare through the

136

main gate into the alley, which was right beside the barn. All at once Cookie gave a snort and started bucking, which was unusual because she had a nice gentle disposition.

I followed her, leading Reno, and at about the same spot, he pitched a fit. I looked around for some kind of booger that might have caused such a reaction in the horses, expecting to find a paper cup or a bread wrapper. I didn't see a thing.

"Well, that's a horse for you," I thought. You never knew what crazy notion a horse might come up with, and you could drive yourself nuts trying to give a rational explanation to his irrational behavior. I thought no more about it.

But later that morning we drove some weaner calves down to the end of the alley, and I noticed that they were acting a little crazy too. They were so stirred up, we could hardly do anything with them.

But again, I thought no more about it—until we got another rain, maybe two weeks later. I went down to the barn and was going through the gate and happened to touch the tin on the side of the barn.

I got an electric shock. From the barn!

I reached down and touched the wet ground, and felt a tingle of electricity. And then I understood why the horses had started bucking when they'd walked through the gate. When the ground was wet, the barn and the area around it were electrified.

Well, that was a new one on me, and I called an electrician to check it out. The best we could figure, the lightning strike had done something to the underground cable that ran from the barn to the bunkhouse, causing a short that didn't show up when the ground dried out, but which came back every time it rained.

The electrician shook his head over this deal. "That's not supposed to happen, but I've learned over the years that electricity does just about what it wants to do, never mind what I think about it."

At any rate, we ran new cable from the barn to the bunkhouse and that put a stop to it.

Up there in Beaver County, the big social event of the week occurred on Wednesday at the Beaver Livestock Auction. On that day all the cowboys and farmers in five counties stopped what they were doing and came out of the sandhills and gathered at the sale barn.

Not long after we moved to Beaver County in 1974, I developed the habit of going to the sale every week, sometimes to peddle some cull cows or pick up an adoption calf for a first-calf heifer, but most often just to enjoy the pageantry of men and livestock.

One day in 1976 the men who ran the sale, Pack Hibbs and Lloyd Barby, came up shorthanded back in the yards and asked if I would con-sider helping them. This was horseback work and I've always had a weak-ness for such folly, so I helped them out.

I must have done all right because they asked me to come back the next week, and then to help them on a regular basis. It was pleasant work that gave me an opportunity to learn the sale barn business, and it paid a little bit, so I became a regular hand, penning cattle as they came off the scales.

One Wednesday in March of 1977, I was working back in the yards. The morning had begun as a still, pleasant, warmish kind of a day; a bit too cool for spring but holding the promise of spring. But around two o'clock, after the sale had been going on for an hour, the wind shifted around and began howling out of the northwest. It got stronger by the hour, and by three o'clock the sun had vanished behind a cloud of dust.

By four o'clock it had gotten so dark that someone inside the auction barn turned on the yard lights—a nice gesture, but the lights didn't help much. The dust was so thick that we couldn't see the top of the grain elevator nearby, or see from one end of the yards to the other.

The wind screamed and roared in the tops of the trees, while Bobby Woodson and I buttoned up our coats, pulled our hats down to our ears, and tried to do the job we'd been hired to do.

That wasn't easy. The wind made our horses nervous and kept the cattle in a constant frenzy, and of course we had some difficulty seeing through the swirl of alley dust, dried manure, and stems of hay that filled the air.

We were all glad when that day came to an end.

It turned out to be quite a storm, the likes of which I haven't seen since. It reminded me a good deal of the big dusters we had during the drought of the 1950s, only the dust in the 1977 storm was not of local origin. It had come from somewhere north of us, eastern Colorado or maybe even from Wyoming.

As I recall, the weather experts explained the storm by saying that a strong low pressure system had sucked the dust high into the air and carried it southward—and by the way, it didn't stop in our country. That same cloud of dust went all the way to the Gulf of Mexico and gave the folks in New Orleans a rare glimpse of a real dust storm.

The wind howled into the night, but by morning it had died down to nothing. I'll never forget the eerie feeling that came over me that morning when I walked out on the front porch and looked off to the south.

Our house was located on a hill and faced the four-section west pasture. The day was bright and absolutely still, and everything I could see was coated with a layer of fine powdery dust that was about the color and consistency of flour or masonry cement.

Off in the distance, maybe a mile away, I could see four or five cows walking in single file towards a windmill. Every time their feet touched the ground, they created a puff of dust. And then when one of them bumped against a sagebrush, it looked as though it had exploded. As more cattle began moving around and going to water, more of those white clouds rose in the still air, until it look as though the whole pasture was on fire.

That was a strange sight.

In the fall of 1981 I was doing some carpentry work at a location about seven miles southeast of Perryton. One warm, still day in October I was eating lunch outside and happened to look up and notice something unusual. The air was filled with what appeared to be thousands of pieces of spider web, varying in length from about six inches up to two or three feet.

They were floating in the air from ground level up to a height of several hundred feet, and they were moving from north to south. The odd thing about these webs was that they were so fine, you couldn't see them in direct sunlight. I had worked outside all morning and hadn't noticed them, but now, by shading my eyes with a hand, I could see them by the thousands.

Throughout the afternoon I would stop my work, shade my eyes, and look up. The webs were still there, floating and twisting and turning in the air. Once the sun went down, it created the kind of indirect lighting on a large scale that I had produced by shading my eyes with my hands. And all at once I could see that everything standing above the ground was covered with those webs—weeds, fence posts, barbed wire, power lines, and highway signs.

What were they? What made them? Where did they come from, and why were they floating in the air? How could millions of strands of "something" go from ground level to a height of fifty or a hundred feet in the air?

I don't know. I haven't seen it happen since then and I've never run across anyone who could explain it.

In the summer of 1987 I drove over to Lipscomb County to spend a couple of days helping Frankie McWhorter with some pasture work on the Gray ranch.

We saddled a couple of horses and trailered over to one of his pastures west of Higgins, unloaded and began counting steers in the sandhills. Accompanying us on this expedition was Frankie's constant companion, a red roan Australian dingo cowdog named, of all things, Hank.

As we rode along, old Hank was out in front of us, sniffing out the country for rabbits. All at once we heard a dog barking. It was a high-pitched kind of a bark. Frankie stopped his horse and listened.

That wasn't Hank's bark. We could see him, maybe fifty yards ahead of us. He had his head up, listening and looking towards the southwest. The barking came again, and this time we were able to follow the sound to a sandhill off to our right. There, standing in plain sight on top of the hill, was a coyote.

He was looking directly at Hank and it was clear that he wanted to get Hank's attention—and that he wasn't the least bit interested in or afraid of Frankie and me.

He barked again, and this time Hank went bounding over to the hill. As he approached, the coyote humped up and bristled. I would guess that Hank had received a good ranch education on the subject of coyotes, and had seen first-hand what sorts of things they do when they're humped up and bristled.

He didn't go charging into the middle of the coyote, but stopped some twenty feet away and began barking. The coyote barked back and took a few steps forward.

Hank ran and the coyote gave chase. After a minute or two of this, the coyote veered off. All at once Hank's courage returned and he became the pursuer.

This was fun to watch. We had no idea what that crazy coyote was doing, whether he was playing or trying to lure Hank into an ambush, but he appeared to be making sport out of it.

He would lope along, glancing back over his shoulder and keeping an eye on old Hank, who had gotten very serious about this chasing business all of a sudden. When the dog got too close, the coyote would turn on a little burst of speed and put some distance between them.

Whether Hank knew it or not, that coyote was making him look pretty silly.

This must have gone on for ten minutes, during which time Frankie and I shifted our positions to keep Hank in sight, just in case he should happen to get himself jumped and mugged.

There's no way that coyote could have not seen us and smelled us, because there were times when he came within fifty feet of us. But he showed no more interest in us than if we'd been a couple of plum bushes.

Up and down the hills they went, the coyote loping along in the lead and, it seemed to us, laughing at Hank over his shoulder, while the Head of Ranch Security was putting his heart and soul into the chase and giving it his most sincere effort.

After a while Frankie said we had to get back to work, so we rode down and ran the coyote off. Poor old Hank, his tongue was a foot long by then, and he had to sit down amidst the sagebrush to catch his wind.

We never did figure out what that coyote was up to. Frankie thought it might have been a she who had a litter of pups nearby, but when we rode out the immediate area, we found no sign of a den. I had seen dogs and coyotes test each other out in the pasture on many occasions, but I had never seen anything quite as brazen as this. Nor had I ever seen a coyote show so little fear in the presence of a man.

It remained a puzzle. Maybe the answer was as simple as why some humans watch boxing on tv or pick fights with their wives: they just get bored.

It was about a year later that I found myself back at Frankie's place, this time to help him shuffle some heifers around and gather up some Angus bulls that had strayed into the wrong pastures.

The last time I'd helped Frankie, he had ridden Bernie, his number one pasture horse, and I had ridden a big brown horse named Billy.

Billy was a pretty good pasture horse and he could take care of his business, but when he moved in a trot he would shake the fillings out of your teeth. Oh, he was rough!

I must have made some comment about Billy and the backache he had given me last time, because when Frankie caught the horses that morning, he handed me Bernie's reins.

Now, that was a surprise. I knew that Frankie ranked Bernie near the top of all the horses he had ridden in his lifetime, and I was properly honored to be given a chance to ride him.

We saddled up. Since we hadn't hooked up the stock trailer yet, I led the two horses over to the trailer while Frankie backed the flatbed pickup under the gooseneck hitch. The trailer was parked in the horse pasture, right beside one of those big overhead storage bins that hold bulk feed. While Frankie struggled with the hitch and muttered unkind things about it, I stood nearby, holding the reins of the two horses while they grazed.

All at once, *Bernie fell to the ground.* I turned and stared at him in disbelief. He hadn't tripped or stumbled. One moment he had been grazing, and now he was lying on his side on the ground!

He fell in such a way that his back legs went under the steel legs of the storage bin. He began thrashing about, trying to get back on his feet, and in the process he kicked the angle iron legs several times.

I could see that if his thrashing worked him farther under the storage bin, when he stood up he would catch a piece of angle iron right in the middle of his back. That would either damage his back or take the cantle off my old Heiser saddle—or maybe both.

I just stood there, watching. I had a feeling that there was probably some clever response to this problem, but I sure didn't know what it was. So I watched and waited to see how much of the ranch Bernie was going to flatten before he got himself out of this wreck.

These problems with horses happen very fast, you know, and sometimes you hear a little voice in your head, discussing the situation as a commentator might discuss a football game. My voice-in-the-head came on about then, and here's what it said:

"Son, we still don't know what you did to cause Bernie to fall down, but we do know that Frankie trusted you with his number one pasture horse. And if Bernie gets himself boogered up, *Frankie is going to cut your heart out and feed it to the buzzards.*"

Bernie kicked and lunged and threw his head around. The angle iron clanged and rang like a bell. I sweated and turned paler by the second. Then at last, he wallowed to his feet without destroying the storage bin, my saddle, or himself. I whistled under my breath and thanked my lucky stars. By that time, Frankie had jumped off the flatbed. "What in the world happened?"

"Frankie, I don't have any idea, honest. One minute he was grazing and the next thing I knew, he was on the ground. I don't think I did anything to cause it."

"No, I don't think you did." He walked up to Bernie and checked him out. When he turned back to me, a little smile was tugging at the corners of his mouth. "I know what happened."

What happened was that while Bernie was grazing, his throat pressed against the breast collar on my saddle, which cut off the flow of blood to his brain. After a minute or so, he blacked out.

The old fool had fainted!

I was amazed. I had never heard of such a thing. Frankie said he'd seen it happen a few times before, once while a man was in the saddle.

You can be sure that I put that one down on my list of Things To Remember About Horses. Never again will I allow a horse to graze when he's wearing a breast collar—especially if his name is Bernie.

Here's another oddity that I rode upon when I was working for the Ellzey family in 1980. It was late summer, as I recall, and we had begun receiving fresh cattle for wheat pasture. We'd gotten in a load or two of steers and bulls from Tennessee and had turned them out in the home section.

We'd had some sickness in these cattle and were watching them closely for Galloping Pneumonia. Tom and I rode them twice a day.

Well, one morning I came up one short on my count. I rode the home section from one end to the other, checking out all the usual spots where sick steers went to hide and commit suicide. By that time I knew all their hiding spots.

But I didn't find my steer, so I began prowling the adjoining pastures. One of these belonged to the Parnell brothers, Tee and Wallace, who joined us on the south. This pasture was known locally as the McClanahan Place, after a family that had owned it many years before.

I had never had occasion to ride that pasture before, so it was all new to me. I rode out the open country on the east and found a couple of Parnell herd bulls, but no steer. So I rode west and entered the country that lay on both sides of Northup Creek.

Obviously the Parnell boys hadn't stocked this pasture very heavily in years, because all that bottom country was overgrown with tall grass, weeds, and sunflowers that were taller than a man on horseback. And above all that were tall trees draped with hanging vines.

We didn't have a great deal of timber in our country, which tended to be flat or rolling. Along Wolf Creek we had stands of cottonwood, native elm, hackberry, china berry, and creek willows, but nothing to compare with the jungle I had found on Northup.

I got out in the middle of that mess and realized that if my steer had gotten in there, he would be granted his wish to die, because I wasn't going to find him. In fact, I had begun to wonder if I would be able to get my horse out.

I was riding along, trying to part the vines and sunflowers with my hands, while Deuce stumbled along, trying to find the ground with his feet, when all at once I looked up and found myself staring into the eyes of a great horned owl. He was maybe ten feet to my right, and *he was hanging upside-down from a limb of a cottonwood tree.*

I stopped my horse and studied on this deal. The owl stared at me and I stared at him. He didn't seem particularly bothered by my presence. He didn't thrash or try to get away. He just hung there and occasionally blinked his big moon eyes.

Why would an owl hang upside-down from a tree limb? That was a new one on me. It appeared that he had gotten one foot tangled up in some vines, so probably he wasn't in his present position by choice.

I considered riding over and helping him out, but the longer I thought about that, the more it sounded like a real bad idea. Owls have these talons, you see, and what they can do to a mouse they can also do to a cowboy's hand, wrist, or nose.

Furthermore, I had reason to suspect that Deuce wouldn't stand still for any mission of mercy that got him thrashed by owl wings, and the thought of riding a bucking horse through that jungle pretty well settled the matter.

I bid Mr. Owl good afternoon and went on my way. I hoped that he would get himself out of that fix, and I imagine that he did.

Ten years later, when I was working on the eleventh Hank the Cowdog book, called *Lost In The Dark Unchanted Forest*, I wrote a scene where Hank happens upon Madame Moonshine, the witchy little owl, hanging upside-down from a tree.

Some people might think that an owl would never get himself in such a predicament and that I came up with the whole thing out of my imagination. But I didn't. It was something I had seen with my own eyes—one of those odd things a cowboy sees once in a lifetime.

Index